Amazing
Dog
Facts and Trivia

"In order to really enjoy a dog, one doesn't merely try to train him to be semihuman. The point of it is to open oneself to the possibility of becoming partly a dog."
Edward Hoagland

Amazing Dog
Facts and Trivia

A canine compendium of tail-wagging trivia

Ryan O'Meara

CHARTWELL
BOOKS, INC.

A QUARTO BOOK

Published in 2010 by
Chartwell Books, Inc.
A division of Book Sales, Inc.
276 Fifth Avenue Suite 206
New York, New York 10001
USA

Reprinted 2011 (twice)

Copyright © 2010 Quarto Inc.

All rights reserved. No part of this
publication may be reproduced,
stored in a retrieval system, or
transmitted in any form or by any
means, electronic, mechanical,
photocopying, recording, or
otherwise, without the permission
of the copyright holder.

ISBN-13: 978-0-7858-2642-2
ISBN-10: 0-7858-2642-4

Conceived, designed,
and produced by
Quarto Publishing plc
The Old Brewery
6 Blundell Street
London N7 9BH

QUA: DGL

Editor & designer:
Michelle Pickering
Art director: Caroline Guest
Indexer: Dorothy Frame

Creative director: Moira Clinch
Publisher: Paul Carslake

Color separation by Modern Age
Repro House Ltd, Hong Kong
Printed by Midas Printing
International Ltd, China

Contents

The contents of this book are completely random, so that each time you open it, you will discover an amazing variety of facts and trivia about the canine world. If you wish to locate a particular category of information, however, this contents listing is organized into topics. There is also an index at the end of the book.

Introduction 8

INTRODUCTION

I have yet to experience anything in life to match the unbridled joy that comes upon being greeted by an animal whose every discernible trait of body language is thrust forth in a wild and public display of sheer, unconditional love.

They say that a dog has lots of friends because it wags its tail more than its tongue. True, no doubt, but that is only a small part of the dog's allure and charm. As domestic animals go, none has been able to match the rise and rise of the canine. From its wolf ancestors, the dependable dog has established its position as the world's most popular companion animal. The dog has earned the title of man's best friend through centuries of devotion, companionship, dedication, courage, and willingness to be whatever we want or need.

Whether you love Samoyeds or Siberian Huskies, Labradors or Leonbergers, this is the perfect book for all dog lovers. On the following pages, you can find out everything you have ever wanted to know about our legendary best friend, as well as lots you probably never thought to ask. Discover why and how the wolf became the domestic dog, and just how new dog breeds are created. Find out how powerful a dog's nose really is, and why most dogs love putting their heads out of car windows. You will find information on the world's most popular dog breeds, plus some you might never have heard of. There are lots of dog care tips, from training techniques to dog-proofing your home, plus amazing canine statistics, from the world's smallest dog to the largest.

This book is an eclectic celebration of the world's most successful animal—our friend, the dog.

As a wise person once said: "In a perfect world, every dog would have a home and every home would have a dog."

What Is a Dog Breed?

How did we arrive at Afghans, Airedales, and Alaskan Malamutes when all we started with was the good old-fashioned wolf? What exactly is a dog breed?

✦ A dog breed can be defined as a group of dogs that share physical and behavioral qualities that humans have selected and refined through breeding.

✦ A dog breed is not a different subspecies—the Yorkshire Terrier is the exact same species as the Great Dane, despite the clear differences in their physical appearance and character.

DOGGY LINGO
- Bitch = Female dog (the male dog is simply called a dog)
- Stud = Male dog used for breeding
- Sire = Male parent
- Dam = Female parent
- Whelp = Newborn puppy
- To whelp = To give birth

Same species? Are you sure? Hmmm, I'm not convinced.

The Yorkshire Terrier is adventurous and fearless, despite its diminutive size.

The statuesque Great Dane is good-natured, playful, and easy to train.

KENNEL COUGH

☆ *Kennel cough is a highly contagious dry, hacking cough. Like the common cold in humans, kennel cough spreads easily from animal to animal, especially when kept in close quarters such as a kennel—hence the name.*

☆ *Kennel cough is caused by several different airborne bacteria and viruses. The veterinarian may treat the cough with antibiotics and cough suppressants, and the affected dog must be kept in quarantine within the home until fully recovered. Disinfect the dog's living areas and keep them well-ventilated.*

☆ *It is possible to give dogs partial protection against some of the causes of kennel cough through vaccination.*

🐴 Canine Population

✱ Recent studies indicate that the canine population is increasing quickly. The total dog population of the world is estimated to be around 400 million dogs. In the United States alone, over 5 million puppies are born each year.

✱ The two countries with the highest dog populations are the United States and France, with an average of one dog per three families.

✱ The two countries with the fewest number of canine pets are Switzerland and Germany, with an average of one dog per ten families.

Did You Know?
There are more dogs in London, England, than there are people in Norway.

CAESAR'S WARNING

Julius Caesar (100–44 B.C.) reportedly had to remind the citizens of Rome to pay more attention to their children and less to their dogs, because the devotion to dogs was so intense.

Taming the Wolf

+ All dogs are scavengers by nature, like their relatives the jackal and coyote. The same is true of the dog's ancestor, the early wolf, which found easy pickings in the waste dumps near human settlements.

+ Just as wolves found benefits from living near humans, humans also saw characteristics in the wolf that would be of great help to them, such as the wolf's superior sense of smell when hunting. It is believed that humans gradually began to breed the animals for particular traits, such as tameness, thereby beginning the process of domestication.

+ As selective breeding became more widely practiced by humans—to perpetuate desirable traits, such as strong guarding instincts or keen eyesight for hunting, for example—this led to the development of the hundreds dog breeds that we have today.

Canis lupus—the wolf.

1 поша
1 ст
НР БЪЛГАРИЯ
1977
Вълк Canis lupus

All dogs are thought to descend from wolves. Both animals are highly social and share many behavioral traits.

PAWS FOR PURPLE HEARTS

❋ Paws for Purple Hearts is a program for military veterans with post-traumatic stress syndrome to train companion and assistance dogs. The act of training and living with the dog is therapeutic to the trainers, and the end result is a well-trained assistance dog for other veterans with physical disabilities.

❋ The dogs are trained to carry out a variety of tasks, such as switching lights on and off, fetching and carrying things, or helping to pull or push a wheelchair. The needs of the veterans are hugely varied, so the training of each animal is specifically matched to particular requirements.

The Purple Heart is awarded to soldiers wounded or killed in action.

Terriers

✦ Terriers derive their name from the Latin word *terra*, meaning "earth." Terriers were bred to locate the den or set of a target animal, such as a badger, rat, or rabbit, either above or below ground, and then bolt, capture, or kill the animal. Terriers have a strong voice for working in the fields with their master.

✦ Popular breeds of terrier include the Yorkshire Terrier, West Highland White Terrier, Staffordshire Bull Terrier, and Lakeland Terrier.

✦ Energetic, sporting, and sometimes noisy, most terriers are affectionate by nature, but they can be nippy.

West Highland White Terrier, or Westie.

Ouch! Dog Bites

The average dog can bite down with an astonishing 150–200 pounds of pressure per square inch (68–91 kg per 2.5 cm), which can cause severe damage. Some larger dogs are capable of producing 450 pounds of pressure per square inch (204 kg per 2.5 cm).

The German Shepherd Dog's bite force has been measured at 238 pounds per square inch (108 kg per 2.5 cm).

DOG WHISPERERS

✣ "Dog whisperer" is the term used to describe a person who is highly attuned to the mind, emotions, instincts, and behavior of dogs. A dog whisperer excels at communicating with dogs.

✣ By using the dog whispering technique in dog training, an environment is created in which the dog can learn without being intimidated or forced to achieve under threat. The process is motivational, non-violent, and based on repetition and positive reinforcement that replicates how dogs react to one another. The dog learns all the training signals, regardless of how subtle they appear.

A dog whisperer applies dog psychology to train dogs.

Doggy Style

The Big Dogs clothing company produces hundreds of T-shirts that portray dogs with humorous sayings.

Finding a Veterinarian

* When choosing a veterinarian, word of mouth is a good place to start, so be sure to ask friends and family for recommendations. Ask them why they chose the veterinarian that they use now.

* Check the veterinarian's connections to local medical associations. See what exactly they are doing to maintain their license.

* If money is a concern, check the veterinarian's prices. Some veterinarians charge more than others, so it can be worth shopping around.

* Once you have selected several veterinarians that you like, schedule a visit to check them out. Ask them about your specific breed of dog, or about any unusual conditions that your dog has. Also, find out what other services are provided, such as grooming or boarding.

Make sure that your dog is comfortable with the veterinarian— this is very important.

Are You Ready for a Dog?

There are many things to be considered before you get a dog. Yes, they are cute and cuddly and will be your new best friend, but dogs also have needs that you must be prepared to meet. Getting a dog is much like having a child—a dog will need care, attention, and discipline just like a child does. You will also have to make changes to your life and your home to make sure that the dog is safe and well cared for. If you are considering getting a dog, ask yourself the questions below to help you make a decision.

Choose a dog that suits your lifestyle. Breeds such as the Labrador Retriever need plenty of exercise.

❶ Do you have enough time?

Dogs are very social animals, and will not be happiest if they are left alone in the backyard all the time. Dogs are happiest when they are included in the family pack. You will need plenty of time to play with and exercise the dog properly. It will also take time to develop a bond of trust with your new pet, and to train it to be well behaved.

❷ Do you have enough space?

A dog needs room at home to run and play, even if you take it on long walks several times a day. Consider carefully what kind of breed will best suit the space you have—a Great Dane is not a wise choice if you live in a small one-bedroom apartment, for example.

Dogs are social animals and enjoy company—canine or human.

PAVLOV'S DOG

Russian scientist Ivan Pavlov (1849–1936) is famous for his experiments in classical conditioning with dogs. Pavlov found that his dogs salivated when they smelled their food on its way. For his experiments, their mealtime was always signaled, such as with the ringing of a bell. After a time, the dogs would salivate in response to the bell alone, even if no food was offered. Pavlov's research into conditioned reflexes helped to advance the understanding of animal and human physiology and neurology.

Ivan Pavlov

DOG SUPPLIES

★ Dog food and treats
★ Food and water bowls
★ Leash, collar, and name tag
★ Toys and chews
★ Dog bed or kennel
★ Grooming tools
★ Carrier and/or crate

Pavlov conditioned his dogs to salivate in response to a signal, such as a bell.

A Boston Terrier with supplies.

❸ Can you afford to become a dog owner?

Dogs can be expensive. The average dog lives around 10–13 years, and the cost of owning a healthy dog for 10 years is around $12,000 (£8,300). Dogs need food, and the larger the dog, the more it eats. Dogs also need collars, leashes, food and water bowls, toys, and so on. If you are getting a puppy, you will probably want to get a crate as well, and will need toilet-training supplies. Some places also require dog owners to get a license. This can usually be obtained by your veterinarian, but will cost a yearly fee. Other costs include trips to the veterinarian, grooming fees, and behavior classes.

The bigger the dog, the more expensive it will be to feed.

IDITAROD TRAIL SLED DOG RACE

❧ The Iditarod Trail Sled Dog Race, crossing Alaska from Anchorage to Nome, is held annually to commemorate the 1925 diphtheria serum run to Nome, known as the "Great Race of Mercy."

❧ The port of Nome was icebound for several months of the year, and when a diphtheria outbreak began in 1925, time was of the essence to transport the vaccine to Nome. Due to the harsh weather, air travel was too dangerous for the task. Instead, the serum was transported by train and a relay of sled dog teams, running through storms and extreme low temperatures in which some of the dogs froze to death.

❧ About 20 mushers and 150 sled dogs were used to carry the diphtheria serum 674 miles (1,085 km) across Alaska. The antitoxin arrived in time to control the epidemic.

The Iditarod race takes its competitors across an incredible range of Alaskan terrain—mountains, frozen rivers, forests, tundra, and coasts.

BENJI

★ Benji, a small mixed breed dog, was the lead character of several family movies and television shows. The role of Benji was originally played by a dog called Higgins; three other dogs have since played Benji.

★ Benji was always around to help the central characters of the story (generally children) to solve their problems, so that they could have a happy ending.

★ The Benji series includes five movies, from the original *Benji* (1974) to the most recent *Benji Off the Leash!* (2004).

Mixed breed dogs can make wonderful family pets. Dog stars such as Benji help to encourage people to adopt such dogs from shelters.

Why Do Dogs Bury Their Food?

+ Ancient dogs survived on whatever they could scavenge or hunt. If they managed to get more than they could eat in a single meal, they had to make sure that the excess would still be available when they became hungry again. They protected the leftover food by burying it.

+ The temperature in the ground is cooler than in the air, so burying food helps it to stay fresh for longer. It also protects the food from flies, and prevents other animals from finding it.

+ Today, dogs are given their food in portions, so they no longer need to save any for a later meal. However, if they do have excess food, they still have the instinct to bury it in a secluded spot for later.

Dogs enjoy digging, especially to store juicy chews to enjoy later.

Choosing a Breeder

If you decide to get your new dog from a breeder, how can you tell if the breeder is a good one? Here are a few tips to help you choose a responsible breeder with healthy pups.

+ If possible, find a breeder through recommendation. Talk to a local veterinarian and ask him or her for a referral to a reliable breeder. Alternatively, ask a trusted friend who has dogs, or visit local dog shows or breeding clubs.

+ As well as being knowledgeable when answering any questions you may have, one of the signs of a good breeder is that he or she will also ask questions about you. The breeder may ask if you have ever owned a dog before, what breeds of dog you have had, where the dog will be housed, and how much time you will be able to spend with the dog. A reputable breeder will NOT sell a puppy to the first interested party; good breeders want to make sure that their dogs go to good homes. Some breeders may even inspect your home before agreeing to sell you a dog.

+ A good breeder will be happy to show you where the dogs are housed and bred, and should have the breeding parents on-site and available for you to look at. If the breeder is not willing to do these things, look elsewhere. Beware of the breeder that only offers to show you "papers" on the pup and its parents—papers are virtually meaningless, because nearly any dog can be registered for papers.

Choosing a breeder carefully will help ensure that your new pet is healthy and without temperament issues.

+ A good breeder should be able to show you the health records of three to five generations of your pup's ancestors.

A good breeder should be willing to show you a puppy's parents on-site.

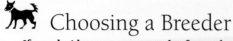

SNUPPY, THE FIRST CLONED DOG

☆ Snuppy, cloned using ear tissue from an Afghan Hound, was born on April 24th, 2005.

☆ Created by scientists at Seoul National University (SNU) in South Korea, Snuppy's name is an amalgamation of "SNU" and "puppy."

☆ Snuppy's sperm was used to inseminate two cloned females—the first known successful breeding of cloned dogs.

☆ *Time* magazine named Snuppy the "Most Amazing Invention of 2005."

The Bloodhound is well-known for its trademark hangdog expression.

Some dog owners now clone their deceased pets

"HANGDOG EXPRESSION"

This phrase is used when someone is expressing their downcast feelings to an extent that you think is excessive, similar to that of a dog sulking after being forbidden to do something.

SMELL THE BREEZE

Dogs have an acute sense of smell, and can detect odors up to 1 million times less concentrated than a human can detect. Their sense of smell is at its greatest when they are moving at speed, which is why so many dogs love to stick their heads out of car windows—they are not looking at the scenery, they are smelling it.

If your dog likes to put its head out of car windows, be aware that there is a risk of injury from airborne debris.

Sniff! Sniff!
Ooo, butcher shop.
Turn around! Please!
Turn around!

Police Dogs

The police dog is not only a highly trained animal, but also a public facet of the police force that many people have come to recognize. Police dogs fulfill various functions.

✦ **Crowd control**—One of the primary roles of the police dog is maintaining public order. They are used to control crowds, most commonly through barking and threatening but controlled behavior. Simply the fear of the dogs being released is normally enough to stop a crowd from advancing on the police.

✦ **On the hunt**—Dogs can outrun people, and are able to jump high fences and other obstacles, making them ideal for chase and capture. Detention is often through biting, but the dogs are trained to do so without causing serious injury. They can also track a criminal by scent after the criminal has left the scene, or they can find a criminal who is hiding on the scene.

✦ **Detection through smell**—Some of the jobs that police dogs are used for rely upon the animal's acute sense of smell in detecting particular odors. The most common use of sniffer dogs is in drug detection. However, they also are used to sniff out explosives and other types of weapons, casualties, and cadavers.

A handler and his German Shepherd Dog compete in the police service dogs event at the World Police and Fire Games, which are held every two years in a different country.

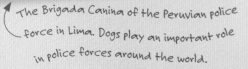

The Brigada Canina of the Peruvian police force in Lima. Dogs play an important role in police forces around the world.

A German Shepherd Dog being trained to hold a suspect by biting an arm, thereby detaining the subject without causing serious harm.

Sniff Power

+ Dogs have almost 50 times more cells that are sensitive to smell than humans. Some breeds, in fact, are specially bred for their smelling capabilities, such as the Bloodhound.

+ Dogs can sense odors at concentrations nearly 100 million times lower than humans can.

Scent hounds have the keenest canine sense of smell, and usually have especially large noses and nostrils.

HIGH-DEFINITION HEARING

★ A dog's sense of hearing is much more attuned than that of humans, and is up to 10 times more efficient than the average human's. Dogs can also hear a much greater frequency range than humans can detect.

★ Dogs have specialized ear shapes that allow them to ascertain where a sound comes from much faster than a human can, and to hear sounds that come from up to four times the distance that humans are able to hear.

★ Eighteen or more muscles can tilt, rotate, and raise or lower a dog's ear.

Oh no, bathtime! Where shall I hide?

Jack Russell Terrier

Dogs are able to move their ears, which helps them to locate the source of sounds.

The Collie's name may share its derivation with the word "coal," because many Collies are predominantly black.

BLACK COLLEY

The name Collie may derive from the Anglo-Saxon word *coll*, which means "black" and is the origin of the word "coal." The name may also come from the word "colley," a name for the Scottish Blackface sheep that the dog was used to herd.

Border Collie

Scottish Blackface sheep, or colley.

September 11th awareness ribbon.

SEPTEMBER 11TH

❋ Within a matter of hours of the September 11th, 2001, attacks on the World Trade Center in New York, a team of specially trained search and rescue dogs were on the scene to lend a hand.

❋ Over 300 dogs of all kinds—mixed breeds, Dachshunds, a variety of Labradors, Collies, German Shepherd Dogs, and Rottweilers—aided in the rescue efforts.

❋ One dog, in particular, stood out from the bunch. Appollo, a German Shepherd service dog from the K-9 unit of the New York Police Department, was the first dog on the scene. Appollo nearly lost his own life when hit by falling debris that engulfed him in flames, and in 2002 received numerous recognitions for his courageous work.

Over 300 dogs, including Appollo the German Shepherd Dog, helped in the search and rescue.

Obedience Training

+ A dog's ability to respond to commands from humans is an aspect of canine intelligence called working/obedience intelligence. It is this characteristic that makes the dog useful for jobs in the human domestic environment. This aspect of the dog's intelligence is based on what the dog can learn through obedience training conducted by a human.

+ Obedience training ranges from basic housetraining to high-level competition training and military training. Obedience connotes compliance with direction or command. A dog can go through obedience training and not be obedient. To be obedient trained, a dog should follow all directives and commands issued by its handler.

Dogs with their owners during an obedience training session.

OBEDIENCE COMMANDS

The following is a list of commonly used voice commands for dog obedience training.

1) "Sit"—To make the dog sit down.

2) "Stand"—To bring the dog up on all four feet.

3) "Stay"—To keep the dog in either the sitting or standing position.

4) "Come"—To bring the dog to the owner.

5) "Down"—To make the dog go to the ground, lying face down.

6) "Heel"—To make the dog walk alongside the owner, traditionally on the left side.

7) "No"—To let the dog know that it has done something wrong.

8) "Fetch" or "Take it"—To make the dog take an object from either the ground or the hand.

9) "Find it" or "Look for it"—To make the dog seek an object that it recognizes by smell, such as tracking or seeking a lost article.

10) "Hup"—To make the dog jump.

It is standard practice to teach a dog to walk on the left-hand side of its owner, known as walking to heel.

HAND SIGNALS

Hand signals are an important part of the dog trainer's repertoire, and should be used in conjunction with voice commands. If you use hand signals correctly, your dog will learn a separate hand signal for every command. There is no standard set of hand signals, but commonly used ones include an outward palm to indicate "Stay" and a lowered palm to indicate "Down." Eventually, the hand signals can be used alone, so choose signals that you can live with.

A young girl using voice commands and hand signals to obedience train her Alaskan Klee Kai puppy.

Gundogs or Sporting Breeds

+ This group of dogs includes pointing breeds (pointers and setters), flushing dogs (spaniels), and retrievers. They were originally bred to assist the hunter in finding, flushing, and retrieving game, usually birds, either on land or in water. Many of the breeds are capable of doing more than one job.

+ Gundogs are active dogs that require plenty of exercise and attention. Popular gundog breeds include Irish Setters, Weimaraners, and Labrador Retrievers.

+ Gundogs make great companions and family dogs. Usually gentle natured, many gundogs have the dual role of hunter's dog and family pet.

+ Some breeds in this group, notably the pointers, remain primarily hunting dogs, whereas others, such as the Golden Retriever, have been more successful in making the transition to family pet.

Pointers and setters help hunters to locate prey.

Spaniels are used to flush game from its hiding place.

РУССКИЙ ОХОТНИЧИЙ СПАНИЕЛЬ

20к

МОСКВА CCCP

1988

Gundogs such as the Golden Retriever were bred to retrieve killed prey and return it to the hunter without further damage.

PUPPY MILLS

- A dog breeding facility that breeds dogs with little or no concern for welfare or good breeding practices, usually primarily for profit, is often referred to as a puppy mill or puppy farm. Smaller puppy mills may be referred to as backyard breeders.
- The concern with puppy mills is that, in order to maximize profits, animal welfare conditions may be substandard, with inadequate food, water, living space, and health care.
- Puppy mills may breed the dogs indiscriminately, with no concern for health or pedigree quality. Females may also be bred every time they go into heat, leading to smaller litters, at which point the females are discarded.
- In recent years, some countries have passed tougher legislation to regulate pet breeders. However, animal welfare activists claim that the legal requirements and inspections are inadequate, and do not prevent puppy mills from operating.

Take care to choose a reputable breeder when buying a dog, such as this Great Dane puppy.

DOG WITCHES?
In the Middle Ages, dogs were often tried and punished along with their owners. Two dogs were hanged in Salem, Massachusetts, in 1692 for witchcraft.

WARNING SIGNS OF A PUPPY MILL

- *If the breeder will not allow you to come on-site to pick up your new puppy or see its parents.*
- *If the breeder is willing to ship the dog to you without meeting you.*
- *If the breeder does not make you sign a contract or offer to take the dog back if things do not work out.*
- *If the breeder does not require you to fill out a screening application or ask for references.*
- *If the breeder is unable to answer any questions you have about the breed and the parents of the dog you are purchasing.*

Rin Tin Tin

NAME CHANGE

In case its German origins harmed the popularity of the breed as a result of the World Wars, the German Shepherd Dog became known as the Alsatian (after the Alsace region of France) or simply the Shepherd Dog, before eventually reverting to its original name.

✦ Rin Tin Tin was a heroic German Shepherd Dog who starred in stories on the silver screen and television.

✦ The original Rin Tin Tin was a puppy found by an American serviceman in France during World War I. Named after a French puppet, the dog's owner later nicknamed him Rinty.

✦ Rin Tin Tin's first acting role was in the movie *The Man from Hell's River* in 1922, but his first starring role was in the film *Where the North Begins* in 1923. He was often cast as a wolf or wolf/dog hybrid.

✦ Rin Tin Tin was also the star of a radio broadcast that was first called *The Wonder Dog*, but later renamed *Rin Tin Tin*. After the original dog died in 1932, his descendants took over the role.

✦ Along with fellow German Shepherd Dog actor Strongheart, Rin Tin Tin was responsible for a dramatic rise in the popularity of the breed in the 1920s, and it remains one of the most popular breeds worldwide today.

Walk of Fame

Three canine actors have a star on the Hollywood Walk of Fame. These are German Shepherd Dogs Rin Tin Tin and Strongheart, and Rough Collie Lassie.

Originally bred to herd sheep, the German Shepherd Dog also excels as a police, guide, and search and rescue dog.

Nylon leash

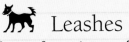

Leashes

There are four main types of dog leash.

+ **Nylon leashes**—These are usually brightly colored and about 6 feet (6 m) in length. Nylon leashes tend to slip through the hands more easily if the dog pulls, and can cut and burn the hand as a result.

+ **Leather leashes**—Leather leashes give you more comfortable control. A good dog trainer can look at a leather leash and tell how much the dog owners are working with their puppies. The more they practice, the softer the leash becomes.

+ **Chain-link leashes**—These are hard on the hands when you move up and down the leash to control the dog. The only good purpose of link leashes is if you need to tie your dog outside for a while—dogs cannot chew through them.

+ **Retractable leashes**—These are mechanically designed to allow the leash to uncoil and travel any distance you allow your dog to run with. The great thing about this leash is that you can stop the distance at any time by simply pressing a lever. You can sit at a park bench and allow your dog to roam at a distance away from you, secure that your pet cannot not escape.

Leather leash

Retractable leash

Retractable leashes allow the dog to walk at a distance, while still giving the owner control.

Cassius Coolidge's paintings have inspired all sorts of memorabilia of poker-playing dogs.

POKER PLAYERS

Cassius Coolidge produced a collection of 16 oil paintings depicting dogs doing human activities, such as dancing and playing baseball, to advertise cigars. Nine of the paintings feature dogs playing poker.

MOST EXPENSIVE BREEDS TO BUY

★ **Havanese:** The Havanese is an extremely rare Cuban toy breed.

★ **Löwchen:** The Löwchen is thought to be the rarest purebred in the world.

★ **Bulldog:** Bulldog puppies are expensive because litters are small and the breed is very popular.

★ **Samoyed:** The Samoyed is a rare but very desirable breed.

★ **Thai Ridgeback:** This breed was unheard of outside Thailand until recently.

★ **Otterhound:** There are less than a thousand of this rare English breed left in the world.

★ **St. Bernard:** This gentle giant is very expensive to buy and to take care of.

Also known as the Little Lion Dog, the expensive Löwchen is traditionally given a lion clip, similar to a Poodle's.

A Havanese puppy is intelligent and affectionate, but also expensive due to its rarity.

BIBLICAL CANINES

Dogs are mentioned in the Bible between 37 and 41 times (depending on the version used). Here are a few examples:

✚ **Exodus 11:7**
"But among the Israelites not a dog will bark at any man or animal." Then you will know that the Lord makes a distinction between Egypt and Israel.

✚ **Exodus 22:31**
You are to be my holy people. So do not eat the meat of an animal torn by wild beasts; throw it to the dogs.

✚ **Judges 7:5**
So Gideon took the men down to the water. There the Lord told him, "Separate those who lap the water with their tongues like a dog from those who kneel down to drink."

✚ **1 Samuel 17:43**
He said to David, "Am I a dog, that you come at me with sticks?" And the Philistine cursed David by his gods.

✚ **1 Kings 14:11**
"Dogs will eat those belonging to Jeroboam who die in the city, and the birds of the air will feed on those who die in the country. The Lord has spoken!"

✚ **2 Kings 8:13**
Hazael said, "How could your servant, a mere dog, accomplish such a feat?" "The Lord has shown me that you will become king of Aram," answered Elisha.

✚ **2 Peter 2:22**
Of them the proverbs are true: "A dog returns to its vomit," and, "A sow that is washed goes back to her wallowing in the mud."

Gustave Doré engraving of Judges 7:5.

FASTEST FIDOS

- Greyhound
- Azawakh
- Whippet
- Saluki
- Borzoi
- Scottish Deerhound

HOUND OF ULSTER

In Irish mythology, the hero Cúchulain slays a fierce guard dog in self-defense and then has to take the dog's place. Known as the Hound of Ulster, he becomes defender of the province for the rest of his life.

The Greyhound can reach speeds of up to 45 miles per hour (72 kph).

JOHN RUSSELL'S TERRIERS

When Reverend John Russell bought a small terrier from his milkman early in the 19th century, he had no idea that he would go on to breed two of the most popular pet dog breeds of the 21st century—the Jack Russell Terrier and the Parson Russell Terrier.

A Jack Russell Terrier (left) and a Parson Russell Terrier.

Dog Intelligence

There are several aspects of human intelligence that can be measured, such as verbal ability, numerical ability, logical reasoning, memory, and so on. Likewise, dog intelligence has different aspects, including three major dimensions.

❶ Instinctive Intelligence

This refers to the dog's instincts specific to its breed. Some dog breeds have the instinctive intelligence to guard or watch over things or to round up livestock; some are bred to retrieve or fetch; some dogs are born to pursue or to track; while companion dogs are more sensitive to human moods and can easily grasp social signals. Each dog has its own instinctive intelligence that should not be compared with dogs of other breeds, because their inherent abilities and intellect are too diverse for comparison.

A herding dog's instinctive intelligence is utilized for rounding up livestock.

❸ Working/Obedience Intelligence

Also called social intelligence, this is the ability of dogs to follow or respond to human instructions or commands. It is the school-learning ability of a dog, and is based upon what the animal can learn from humans.

❷ Adaptive Intelligence

Adaptive intelligence relates to what a dog can learn for itself. This includes its survival instincts and how it can adapt to its environment by learning through experience, solving new problems, facing danger, and so on. Adaptive intelligence can differ among individual dogs of the same breed. While all Golden Retrievers have the same instinctive intelligence, their adaptive intelligence differs, sometimes in very diverse ways. The disparity in adaptive intelligence between dogs of the same breed can be measured by using suitable tests.

A dog's ability to learn from humans is known as working/obedience intelligence.

QUESTIONS TO ASK A BREEDER

Although there are many excellent dog breeders, there are also some who do not produce good-quality, healthy animals. It is important to choose a reputable breeder in order to minimize the risk of your new pet having any health or temperament issues. Here are some questions that a good breeder should be able to answer:

1) What is the goal of your breeding program?

2) How long have you been involved with the breed?

3) What are some of the strong and weak traits of the breed?

4) How old are your puppies before you sell them?

5) Will you accept the dog back if things are not working out, there are health problems, or my situation changes? A reputable breeder will not only say yes, but will require that the dog be returned to them and not taken to a shelter or sold to another owner. This stipulation should be included in the ownership contract from the breeder.

DOGS IN MUSIC VIDEOS

- "Sweet Child O' Mine" by Guns N' Roses features a Rottweiler.
- "Black Hole Sun" by Soundgarden stars a Great Dane.
- "What's My Name?" by Snoop Dogg features a bunch of dogs that morph into gangsters.

Greyfriars Bobby

Greyfriars Bobby is a perfect example of how dedicated and loyal dogs can be. In 1858, Bobby's owner, a nightwatchman named John Gray, died and was buried in Greyfriar's churchyard in Edinburgh, Scotland. The little Skye Terrier found his owner's resting place and guarded it for 14 years, only leaving for food. When Greyfriars Bobby passed away, the dog was honored with a granite fountain in 1873 for dedication to his owner. The dog's story has inspired several books and films.

A statue of Greyfriars Bobby tops a fountain in his honor in Edinburgh, Scotland.

AFRICAN DOG
Almost all dogs are members of the order "Canis lupus familiaris." However, it is sometimes claimed that the Chinese Crested Dog is part of the "Canis africanus" order.

CANINE DIABETES
Canine diabetes causes the same problems as diabetes in humans, and requires similar treatments. Dogs can receive regular insulin shots to help stabilize their blood sugar levels, and there are also some natural supplement treatments that are receiving more and more attention.

The hairless Chinese Crested Dog is ideal for allergy sufferers.

DOG BLESS YOU!
Although no dog is 100 percent hypoallergenic or non-shedding, several breeds yield less dander—flakes of dry skin that are the real cause of allergies. Here are some breeds to consider if you suffer from allergies:

★ Bedlington Terrier
★ Bichon Frise
★ Chinese Crested Dog
★ Irish Water Spaniel
★ Kerry Blue Terrier
★ Maltese
★ Poodle
★ Portuguese Water Dog
★ Schnauzer
★ Soft-coated Wheaten Terrier

Dogs can catch diseases from contact with other animals. Some can be passed onto humans, and are known as zoonoses.

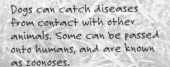

Crufts staff remove over 10 tonnes of dog mess—carpet tiles make clean-up easier.

CLEAN-UP

The 85,000 square foot (7,900 sq m) floor at the (British) Kennel Club's Crufts dog show in England is covered with individual carpet tiles. If the competitors have any accidents, individual tiles can be removed and replaced rather than cleaned, which would take too long.

ZOONOSIS

✳ A zoonosis (or zoonose) is any infectious disease that can be transmitted from animals to humans. Zoonotic diseases are more common and serious in third world countries and tropical climates.

✳ Dogs can be exposed to diseases via contact with other animals or animal droppings. There are more than 60 types of disease that dogs can catch, about 20 of which can be passed onto humans. These include rabies, internal parasites (such as hookworms and tapeworms), fleas, ticks, and mange.

✳ With many zoonotic diseases, humans do not catch the disease directly from the dog. Instead, the animal serves as a barometer, signaling the presence of infectious agents in the environment that humans may also catch.

A toddler
befriends
six-time Crufts
champion
Bloodhound
Lee of
Reynalton
in 1935.

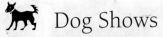

Dog Shows

Dog shows range from small local shows, hosting contests from Waggiest Tail to Handsomest Dog, to major international conformation competitions, where a win of Best in Breed or Best in Show can bring enormous success to the winning dog's breeder or kennel of origin. Dogs need to compete in accredited Championship shows in order to earn points or certification toward winning a Championship title. Only Champions can compete in the major international shows.

CRUFTS

Crufts is the largest annual conformation dog show in the world. Hosted by the (British) Kennel Club in England, entries average 21,000 dogs, judged over the course of four days. Vendors on-site offer an astonishing variety of things to buy—everything from high-quality dog art and collectables to grooming aprons, food, books, and clothing for humans. The Crufts committee provides dog experts to advise prospective and current dog owners on bahavioral, nutritional, and management problems.

WESTMINSTER KENNEL CLUB DOG SHOW

Established in 1877, the most prestigious American dog show is the Westminster Kennel Club Dog Show. Held annually in New York, the show judges more than 2,500 dogs over the course of two days. The show is the centerpiece of a week of educational seminars, lectures, parties, and award dinners.

CHARLES CRUFT

Crufts was founded by Charles Cruft, whose work for a dog biscuit manufacturer entailed traveling to dog shows. He realized that better organized shows could improve the quality of pedigree dogs. His first show in 1886 was advertised as the "First Great Terrier Show," becoming "Cruft's Greatest Dog Show" in 1891.

Surely this will win me the prize for Waggiest Tail. Phew, it's tiring...

WORLD DOG SHOW

Sponsored by the Fédération Cynologique Internationale, the World Dog Show is held in a different country each year. It is only at this show that the title "World Champion" for the year can be awarded.

A Chihuahua wagging its tail.

Breeding Techniques

There are three main methods used for breeding dogs—line breeding, inbreeding, and outcrossing. The merits of each are highly debated among dog lovers and breeders, because each can cause health problems and genetic defects that might not have arisen otherwise.

+ **Line breeding**—This is the process wherein dogs with common ancestors are bred to each other in an attempt to reinforce desired characteristics and eliminate undesirable ones. Typical matings are aunt/nephew, grandfather/ granddaughter, and cousin/cousin—that is, not direct relatives, as used with inbreeding. A good knowledge of genetics is required to carry out line breeding successfully, but sometimes the wrong traits can result because line breeding does not always produce exactly what is expected.

+ **Inbreeding**—This involves the breeding of close relatives—brother/ sister; father/daughter; mother/son—to concentrate desirable traits. Conversely, it also concentrates undesirable ones. Inbreeding is highly controversial, with whole litters sometimes having to be destroyed because of genetic defects. Even the most experienced breeder should not inbreed their dogs continually. However, this method is the only option when trying to repopulate a breed that is close to extinction, or when starting a new dog breed altogether.

+ **Outcrossing**—This method involves breeding two linebred dogs from different lines; they should not share any common ancestry. This introduces greater genetic diversity, but usually results in less uniformity or concentration of positive traits.

A litter of Belgian Tervueren Shepherd Dog puppies that have been linebred to concentrate desirable traits.

Two young Rhodesian Ridgebacks playing. Dogs can transmit viruses to one another via saliva and nasal secretions during play.

CANINE INFECTIOUS HEPATITIS

Canine infectious hepatitis is a disease of the liver, caused by a virus. This virus does not affect humans, but is spread between animals through urine, feces, blood, and nasal and eye secretions. These must contact the dog directly in order to infect it. Symptoms include coughing, fever, and loss of appetite. The virus usually takes from a few days to a couple of weeks to run its course. During this time, antibiotics are usually administered so that secondary infections are avoided. Prevention is by vaccination.

DOG BREEDS NAMED AFTER PLACES

- Afghan Hound
- Alaskan Malamute
- Amercian Cocker Spaniel
- American Foxhound
- Anatolian Shepherd Dog
- Belgian Malinois and Tervueren Shepherd Dogs
- Bernese Mountain Dog
- Black Russian Terrier
- Bouvier des Flandres
- Brussels Griffon
- English Cocker Spaniel
- English Foxhound
- Finnish Spitz
- German Pinscher
- German Shepherd Dog
- German Pointer
- Irish Water Spaniel
- Irish Wolfhound
- Italian Greyhound
- Japanese Chin

TITANIC SURVIVORS

Three dogs are believed to have survived the sinking of the *Titanic* by boarding the lifeboats with their owners. Margaret Hays and Elizabeth Rothschild each took their Pomeranians with them. Henry Sleeper Harper carried his Pekingese, Sun Yat Sen, with him.

Continued on page 44

Give older dogs regular exercise, but do not expect them to manage long walks. With less activity, the dog will also need fewer calories.

Continued from page 43

Dog Breeds Named After Places

- Kerry Blue Terrier
- Labrador Retriever
- Lakeland Terrier
- Maltese
- Newfoundland
- Norwegian Elkhound
- Nova Scotia Duck Tolling Retriever
- Polish Lowland Sheepdog
- Portuguese Water Dog
- Pyrenean Mountain Dog
- Rhodesian Ridgeback
- St. Bernard
- Scottish Deerhound
- Scottish Terrier
- Shetland Sheepdog
- Siberian Husky
- Skye Terrier
- Spinone Italiano
- Sussex Spaniel
- Tibetan Mastiff
- Tibetan Spaniel
- Tibetan Terrier
- Welsh Springer Spaniel
- Welsh Terrier
- Yorkshire Terrier

SIGNS OF OLD AGE

Being aware of some of the common problems that accompany old age will enable you to care better for your dog's health. Problems include:

✤ Deterioration of the teeth.

✤ Obesity as the dog's mobility decreases and it becomes less active.

✤ Behavioral changes, such as being more tired and less willing to exercise or walk.

✤ Walking more slowly, which may indicate arthritis.

✤ Loss of sight or loss of hearing.

BUYING AN OLDER PUREBRED

Look at breed-specific websites and shelters. There is always an abundance of retired breeding dogs and show dogs that are in need of good homes. You can also ask a veterinarian for the name of a reputable breeder. Breeders will often sell older dogs when they are not planning to breed any more litters from them.

"THREE DOG NIGHT"

This phrase originates from the indigenous Aborigines of Australia, who would sleep with their dogs for warmth on cold nights. A very cold night was referred to as a three dog night.

Australia's wild dog, the Dingo, does not bark—it howls.

Hounds

+ Hounds are often divided into two groups: sight hounds and scent hounds.

+ Sight hounds are one of the oldest types of dog. Silent and graceful, they rely on their keen eyesight to spot, hunt, and kill prey—a hunting method known as "coursing." Sight hounds that are commonly kept as pets include Greyhounds, Afghan Hounds, and Whippets.

+ Scent hounds have some of the most sensitive noses among canines, and primarily hunt by scent rather than sight. They hunt in packs, and some have deep, booming barks. Popular scent hounds include Beagles and Basset Hounds.

+ Hounds are good natured, but have a propensity to roam. Many hounds are kept in packs in outside kennels, rather than indoors.

The Beagle has one of the keenest senses of smell of any dog breed.

A Bearded Collie jumping a hurdle in an agility contest. The Beardie is an active dog that enjoys plenty of exercise, making it a great choice as an agility dog.

🐎 Dog Agility

* Dog agility is a very popular dog sport in which a handler directs a dog through an obstacle course. The dogs compete in a race for time as well as accuracy, with penalties being incurred for faults, such as knocking over a hurdle.

* Dogs run the race off-leash, with the handler using a combination of voice and body signals to control the dog. The handler is not allowed to touch the dog or the obstacles, or to persuade the dog with food or toys.

* All dog breeds can enter, although some breeds do excel in the sport, including Shetland Sheepdogs, Border Collies, and Corgis.

* Dogs are divided into categories according to size and experience, with a winner selected in each category.

Leaping through a tire jump—Border Collies excel at agility contests.

AGILITY OBSTACLES

Common agility obstacles include:
• Jumps
• Weave poles
• Ramps
• Tunnels
• Pause tables

A Dalmatian racing through weave poles, which many dogs find difficult to master.

A Pembroke Welsh Corgi emerging from a tunnel. Despite their short legs, Corgis make excellent agility dogs.

WHY DO SOME DOGS EAT POOP?

★ Dogs are natural scavengers, and many dogs will enthusiastically eat feces, known as coprophagia. Some dogs prefer to eat their own droppings or those of other dogs, while others are attracted to the dung of other animals, such as cows or deer.

★ While feces may smell bad to humans, it simply smells tasty to the dog. One theory is that the dog is attracted to the undigested nutrients in the feces. A bored dog may also explore things with its mouth, including dung.

★ A dog may get worms from eating the stools of an infected animal, but generally the habit is unpleasant rather than dangerous. The first recourse should be to check the dog's normal diet to make sure that the dog is getting sufficient nutrients. Also get the dog checked by a veterinarian in case of poor digestion.

★ If there is no clinical reason for the poop eating, then behavioral training can be used to try to stop the habit, including teaching the dog the "Leave" command. Making feces unpleasant for the dog may also help; spray the dung with pepper, which is an irritant when inhaled, and bring the dog near the feces. If the "Leave" command does not work, then the pepper spray should discourage the dog from touching the feces. If the dog eats its own feces, including pineapple or kelp tablets in the dog's diet can make the feces taste unpleasant.

Oh look, rabbits! They always leave a tasty snack behind.

The domestic dog descends from a long line of scavengers, and can find the most unpleasant things tasty.

DOG REPRODUCTION

♥ In domestic canines, sexual maturity (puberty) occurs between the ages of 6 and 12 months for both males and females, although this can be delayed until up to two years of age for some of the larger breeds.

♥ Although small breeds mature sexually earlier than larger breeds, nature has a way of averaging everything—small breeds reproduce younger and live longer than large breeds, but they also have smaller litters.

♥ Pregnancy is possible as soon as the first estrus cycle, but breeding is not recommended prior to the third cycle.

Sexual maturity can occur as early as 6 months of age.

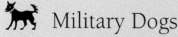

Military Dogs

Dogs have been used by humans for military purposes for thousands of years. In the modern military, some of the jobs dogs have been used for include scout, sentry, tracker, and messenger.

+ **Scout's honor**—A scout dog goes out with its handler in search of information, such as the location of people they wish to find or avoid. Thanks to the dog's sense of smell, both handler and dog can maintain a safe distance.

+ **Sentry service**—The sentry dog is used to prevent unauthorized entry to a place, preferably by being able to spot the oncoming danger long before it reaches the place being guarded.

+ **Trained tracker**—In the past, tracker dogs were used to find and follow the enemy, or to locate missing or injured friendly forces or civilians. The dogs did this by following the scent of the individual, or a scent that was common to the enemy forces. Tracker dogs are no longer used in the military. This role is now carried out by soldiers relying upon visual tracking.

+ **Military messenger**—A messenger dog is trained by two handlers instead of the usual one, so that the dog can be called upon to travel long distances between the handlers. Historically, their primary purpose was to carry information across distances that were unsafe for humans, perhaps because it was enemy territory. Today, they must be able to carry up to 30 pounds (13.6 kg) of ammunition or supplies from one handler to another, which necessitates a relatively sturdy dog to fulfill the role.

A German Shepherd Dog stands sentry with its handler in Afghanistan.

The Dandie Dinmont Terrier makes an affectionate, playful, and intelligent companion.

A WORK OF FICTION

The Dandie Dinmont Terrier is the only dog breed to be named after a fictional character. The original Dandie Dinmont was a "rough but jovial" farmer with a pack of little terriers who appeared in Sir Walter Scott's 1815 novel, Guy Mannering.

From Weasel to Dog

❀ The ancestry of the dog can be traced back 60 million years to a tree-climbing, weasel-like creature called the Miacis, which is thought to have demonstrated the first characteristics of the carnivore with which we are familiar today. The Miacis is the common ancestor of both the cat (Felidae) and dog (Canidae) families.

❀ It is believed that one of the descendants of the Miacis was the Tomarctus, a wolf-like pack animal that appeared about 15 million years ago. This creature is thought to have evolved into the Canis genus that includes jackals, coyotes, and wolves.

❀ Most authorities agree that the wolf, *Canis lupus*, is the dog's most recent ancestor, and the domestic dog is now normally classified as *Canis lupus familiaris*.

Weasel

НР БЪЛГАРИЯ   поща 10 ст

1977 Невестулка Mustela nivalis

The dog's early ancestor, the Miacis, was a weasel-like creature.

The Tomarctus was a pack animal, similar to the dog's most recent ancestor, the wolf.

A pack of gray wolves, the dog's most recent ancestor.

A Border Collie rounds up sheep into an enclosure during a sheepdog trial.

Two dogs work in tandem to herd sheep during a sheepdog trial.

CUSHING'S SYNDROME

❉ *Cushing's syndrome is where the adrenal glands produce an overabundance of the hormone cortisol; too much or too little of this hormone can be deadly. Most often, the cause is a tumor.*

❉ *The syndrome is more common in older dogs, and indeed the symptoms are often mistaken for the normal aging process. Symptoms include hair loss, frequent urination, increased thirst and appetite, and the development of a pot belly.*

❉ *There are several treatment options, such as surgery and medication, depending on the tumor's location and the stage of the disease.*

Sheepdog Trials

+ A sheepdog trial is a competitive dog sport in which herding dogs move sheep around a field; fences, gates, or enclosures, as directed by their handlers.

+ Such events are particularly associated with hilly grass areas. These trials are popular in South Africa, Chile, Canada, the United States, Australia, New Zealand, Britain, Ireland, and other farming nations.

+ Some venues allow only dogs of known herding breeds to compete; others allow any dog that has been trained to work stock. A well-trained dog can fetch a high price, as can its puppies, and can perform amazing feats of stockmanship.

+ There are several events in sheepdog trials, but the key element is the control of three to six sheep by one or two highly trained dogs under the control of a single handler. Both time and obedience play a part, and competitors are penalized if a sheep strays from the prescribed course.

Search and Rescue Dogs

Search and rescue (SAR) dogs are trained to detect the scents of humans, either alive or dead. They may be trained to detect generic human scents, or to discriminate between scents in order to locate specific individuals.

+ SAR dogs fall into two main categories—those that detect any human scent in the air (air-scenting dogs), and those that detect scents from a specific individual (trailing and tracking dogs).

+ Air-scenting dogs follow generic airborne human scents to their source. Trailing and tracking dogs are exposed to an item connected to a missing person, and then follow the person's scent until it stops. Tracking dogs track the exact physical path the person took, utilizing scent and signs of ground disturbance, while trailing dogs follow the scent only, which may have dispersed from the original path.

+ SAR dogs must work under hugely varied conditions, and may face both natural disasters, including earthquakes, landslides, and avalanches, as well as building collapses. All of these conditions are likely to be hazardous, and so dogs that are employed in this way must be very agile.

+ Collapsed buildings, in particular, present high risks, because of the chance of further shifting. The dogs may have to navigate tight spaces and fragile structures to pinpoint the location of any victims, before returning and alerting the handler to where they are.

+ In the case of an avalanche, the dog will have to survive freezing conditions, and be able to climb well. Scents from the people involved are likely to be stifled by the volume of snow above them, requiring a dog with a very sensitive sense of smell.

+ Drowning victims are a special challenge faced by a SAR dog, because of the potential for moving water to cover the scent.

+ SAR work is physically demanding for both dogs and handlers, and the dogs must be able to work for up to 4–8 hours, without becoming distracted by anything around them. The dogs are exposed to possible distractions during training, in order that they will learn to ignore them.

POPULAR SEARCH AND RESCUE BREEDS
- Bloodhound
- German Shepherd Dog
- Newfoundland
- Labrador Retriever

A German Shepherd Dog follows a scent during a search and rescue mission in a desert environment.

A 2,000-year-old Roman floor mosaic warning "Beware of the dog" ("Cave canem" in Latin) in a house in Pompeii, Italy.

Faithful Fido

Fido, the commonly used nickname for a dog, means "I am faithful" in Latin.

BUTCHER'S DOG

✤ The Rottweiler is named after the town of Rottweil in southwest Germany, where the breed originated. The town was named after the red-tiled roofs of Roman buildings that once stood in the town.

✤ In its native Germany, this breed is still referred to as the Rottweiler Metzgerhund (Rottweil Butcher's Dog), because in the past it worked as a draft dog delivering meat.

The Rottweiler has been used as a hunter of wild-boar, a trusted cattle dog, and a butcher's dog.

CHINESE YEAR OF THE DOG

❀ In Chinese astrology, it is believed that each person is governed by one of 12 animal signs, depending on the person's year of birth. The dog governs people born in 2018, 2006, 1994, 1982, 1970, 1958, 1946, 1934, 1922, and 1910 (using the Chinese lunar calendar).

❀ People born in the year of the dog are loyal, responsible, sensitive, moral, trustworthy, and imaginative. Dog people are life's helpers and supporters, always ready and willing to pick up the pieces, lend a shoulder to cry on, entertain and lift the spirits, reassure and give hope, and generally make life a better place for everyone. Dog people are honest and principled, energetic and enthusiastic, generous and kind, and liked and respected.

❀ On the downside, dog people can worry a lot and be too idealistic. Dog people can also be stubborn, appear to be quite nosy, and can be overwhelmingly enthusiastic at times.

❀ Romantically, dog people are particularly compatible with those born in the years of the horse or tiger, as well as other dogs.

Scruffts competitors are judged on character, health, and temperament.

Scruffts

This dog show, named after the famous Crufts show and also run by the (British) Kennel Club, is open to mixed breeds only. All money raised goes to charity.

Calligraphy symbol for the Chinese zodiac sign of the dog.

A traditional Chinese papercut for the zodiac sign of the dog.

PUREBREDS ... AND OTHER COMBINATIONS

❋ *Pureblood is the original term for what we know today as purebred. A purebred is a dog whose parents are both of the same established breed.*

❋ *A crossbreed or crossbred usually refers to a dog with parents of two different established breeds.*

❋ *A mixed breed, commonly referred to as a mongrel, is a dog with ancestry in two or more different dog breeds, or whose genetic heritage is unknown.*

❋ *A dog hybrid is the result of interbreeding between two animals of different species, such as a dog breeding with a wolf or jackal.*

I'm just as lovable as a purebred, aren't I?

A mixed breed, or mongrel.

A purebred French Bulldog.

TEDDY ROOSEVELT TERRIER

The teddy bear was named after Theodore Roosevelt, the 26th president of the United States. So far, he is the only American president to have a dog breed named in his honor. The Teddy Roosevelt Terrier is a relative of the Rat Terrier.

Pregnancy and Litter Size

✦ Pregnancy lasts an average of 63 days from the date of mating, although it can appear to be longer or shorter than this, because sperm can survive in the bitch's reproductive tract for several days before fertilizing eggs. The length of the pregnancy depends on several factors, including how soon fertilization occurred, the size of the dog, and the size of the litter she is carrying.

✦ In dogs, the great range of sizes and shapes plays a role in how many healthy pups a female can carry. An average litter consists of six puppies, although this number may vary widely, depending on the breed of dog. Toy dogs generally produce from one to four puppies in each litter, while much larger breeds may average as many as 14 pups per litter.

✦ Since a mother can provide nutrients and care to a limited number of offspring, humans must assist in the care and feeding when the litter exceeds approximately eight puppies.

FULL LITTER

Some people claim that mating dogs on alternate days is the way to achieve a full litter. Others say that mating every day is much better, because it reduces the chance of one puppy being born prematurely or much later than the other pups of the litter.

A litter of newborn Golden Retriever puppies suckling from their mother.

A Golden Retriever nursing six young puppies—the average number of puppies in a litter.

DOGS IN CHILDREN'S SONGS
- "B-I-N-G-O" (which is the name of a dog)
- "Old MacDonald Had A Farm"
- "Where, Oh Where Has My Little Dog Gone?"
- "(How Much Is) That Doggie In The Window?"

COLOR VISION

★ Like most mammals, dogs are dichromats, which means that they have color vision equivalent to red–green color blindness in humans.

★ Retina configurations and eye shapes and dimensions vary by breed, just like many other physical characteristics in dogs.

The Greyhound was valued for its great speed by the ancient Egyptians.

Biblical Breed: Greyhound or Rooster?

✦ The Greyhound was once the only dog breed mentioned in the Bible. In the King James Version, Proverbs 30:29–31 is translated as: *"There be three things which go well, yea, four are comely in going: A lion which is strongest among beasts, and turneth not away for any; a greyhound; an he goat also; and a king, against whom there is no rising up."*

✦ However, modern translations, such as the New International Version, translate these verses differently: *"There are three things that are stately in their stride, four that move with stately bearing: a lion, mighty among beasts, who retreats before nothing; a strutting rooster, a he-goat, and a king with his army around him."*

✦ "Strutting rooster" is now considered a more accurate translation of the original Hebrew text than "Greyhound."

The stately Greyhound has been replaced by a strutting rooster in modern translations of the Bible.

Lassie with Roddy McDowall in the 1943 movie "Lassie Come Home." During the film, Lassie journeys many miles and overcomes many obstacles in order to return to her beloved young owner.

The name Papillon is French for "butterfly," and comes from the breed's erect ears.

GOOD BREEDS FOR

CITY LIVING

❀ *Chihuahua*

❀ *Pug*

❀ *Shih Tzu*

❀ *Bichon Frise*

❀ *Papillon*

COUNTRY LIVING

❀ *Border Collie*

❀ *Patterdale Terrier*

❀ *Old English Sheepdog*

❀ *Rottweiler*

❀ *Great Dane*

Lassie

✦ One of the most famous heroic dogs of all time is a faithful Collie named Lassie, created by Eric Knight in a short story for the *Saturday Evening Post* in 1938. Knight expanded the story into a novel called *Lassie Come-Home* in 1940.

✦ The book was developed into a screenplay for the 1943 movie *Lassie Come Home*. The lead role of Lassie was played by a male Rough Collie called Pal, who starred alongside Roddy McDowall and Elizabeth Taylor. Pal starred in six sequels to the original film through to 1951.

✦ Lassie was also the star of a television show from 1954 to 1973, one of the longest running television series ever. Pal played the role of Lassie in two pilots for the television show, before retiring and passing the role onto his descendants.

A Labrador Retriever licking a scraped palm.

Lick It Better

It is often said that wounds will heal more quickly if a dog licks them. Unfortunately, this is just a myth.

HOW SMART IS YOUR DOG?

In his 1994 book The Intelligence of Dogs, *Dr. Stanley Coren, a neuropsychologist and professor of psychology at the University of British Columbia in Vancouver, Canada, provided a list of dog breeds ranked according to their working/obedience intelligence—that is, what they can be taught by humans—after he asked more than 200 dog trainers and obedience judges to rank the breeds. Dr. Coren's ranking of breeds is listed below.*

The Border Collie is used as a working sheepdog all over the world.

Top of the class: the Border Collie.

1 Border Collie
2 Poodle
3 German Shepherd Dog
4 Golden Retriever
5 Doberman Pinscher
6 Shetland Sheepdog
7 Labrador Retriever
8 Papillon
9 Rottweiler
10 Australian Cattle Dog
11 Pembroke Welsh Corgi
12 Miniature Schnauzer
13 English Springer Spaniel
14 Belgian Tervueren Shepherd Dog
15 Schipperke
   Belgian Sheepdog
16 Collie
   Keeshond
17 German Shorthaired Pointer
18 Flat-coated Retriever
   English Cocker Spaniel
   Standard Schnauzer

Continued on page 61

DOES DOG INTELLIGENCE MATTER?

❧ Dog breeds have been ranked on the basis of their working/obedience intelligence (what they can be taught by humans), but this is only one aspect of their intelligence. Every dog also has its instinctive (inbred) and adaptive (what they can learn by themselves) intelligence, which guide the dog's behavior and its role in the domestic lives of humans.

❧ Even if a breed ranks low in terms of working/obedience intelligence, this should not eliminate that breed from your choice as a pet. Some dog breeds are excellent as sporting dogs, some are outstanding as working dogs, and some breeds make for a better pet.

❧ Keep in mind that a clever dog may require more training in order to learn the limits of acceptable dog behavior in the family home.

🐕 Dogs in Movies

✦ *Beethoven*, released in 1992, was the first in a series of movies following the adventures of a St. Bernard and its growing family (and owners).

✦ *All Dogs Go to Heaven* (1989) is an animated film telling the story of Charlie, a roguish dog who forfeits his place in heaven in order to return to earth to seek revenge against his murderer. Although Charlie initially continues with his shady schemes, he eventually becomes attached to a young girl and protects her when she is threatened by his own murderer—thereby earning back his place in heaven.

✦ The *Wallace and Gromit* series of "claymation" animated films tell the adventures of a man and his dog. Wallace is an inventor who loves cheese. Gromit is his intelligent dog, whose skills include engineering, electronics, knitting, and cooking. Gromit does not speak, but communicates through facial expressions and body language.

The St. Bernard, star of the "Beethoven" movies, is a gentle giant and loves children.

I love claymation movies. I wonder if I could get a part as Gromit's sidekick...

I wonder if cheese goes with fish...

Continued from page 60

How Smart Is Your Dog?

19 Brittany Spaniel

20 Cocker Spaniel

21 Weimaraner

22 Belgian Malinois Shepherd Dog
    Bernese Mountain Dog

23 Pomeranian

24 Irish Water Spaniel

25 Hungarian Vizsla

26 Cardigan Welsh Corgi

27 Chesapeake Bay Retriever
    Hungarian Puli
    Yorkshire Terrier

28 Giant Schnauzer

29 Airedale Terrier
    Bouvier des Flandres

30 Border Terrier
    Briard

31 Welsh Springer Spaniel

32 Manchester Terrier

33 Samoyed

Continued on page 62

Continued from page 61

How Smart Is
Your Dog?

The FDR Memorial
in Washington, D.C.,
includes a statue of
Fala, the president's
Scottish Terrier.

34 Field Spaniel
Newfoundland
Australian Terrier
American Staffordshire Terrier
Gordon Setter
Bearded Collie

35 Cairn Terrier
Kerry Blue Terrier
Irish Setter

36 Norwegian Elkhound

37 Affenpinscher
Australian Silky Terrier
Miniature Pinscher
English Setter
Pharaoh Hound
Clumber Spaniel

38 Norwich Terrier

39 Dalmatian

40 Soft-coated Wheaten Terrier
Bedlington Terrier
Smooth Fox Terrier

41 Curly-coated Retriever
Irish Wolfhound

42 Hungarian Kuvasz
Australian Shepherd

43 Saluki
Finnish Spitz
Pointer

44 Cavalier King Charles Spaniel
German Wire-haired Pointer
Black and Tan Coonhound
American Water Spaniel

🐎 Presidential Dogs

+ Franklin D. Roosevelt's Scottish Terrier, named Fala, accompanied him almost everywhere. Fala is buried next to Roosevelt, and there is a statue of him at the Franklin Delano Roosevelt Memorial in Washington, D.C.

+ George and Barbara Bush's English Springer Spaniel Millie inspired a children's book entitled *Millie's Book: As Dictated to Barbara Bush*, about Millie's litter of puppies.

+ Barack Obama promised his daughters a new dog after his presidential campaign. Their new pet, Bo, was a Portuguese Water Dog.

DIABETIC DETECTION DOGS

Diabetic detection dogs are used to detect the distinct odor given off by a diabetic person whose blood sugar level is dropping. The dog then alerts someone who can help. Children, in particular, may not notice that their blood sugar is dropping until it is too late, but the dog can alert the parents before the condition becomes life threatening.

Continued on page 64

Shelter Dogs

A wonderful place to get a dog from is your local animal shelter. Every year, thousands of dogs are placed in shelters to await adoption by a new family. There are many excellent reasons to choose a shelter dog as a new pet.

* By getting a shelter dog, you are giving a dog a new chance at having a great life.

* Shelters have a wide variety of dog breeds of all ages, as well as plenty of mixed breeds. Shelters may have puppies as well as older dogs, because some people give up pregnant dogs or take whole litters to the shelter because they cannot afford to take care of them.

* Many dogs in shelters are a year old or more, so they may already be housetrained. By choosing an older dog from a shelter, you can see exactly what you are getting as far as size, appearance, and grooming requirements are concerned.

* Most shelters screen the dogs for temperament before placing them for adoption. This usually entails seeing how a dog interacts with people, children of varying ages, other dogs, and cats.

* Shelters vaccinate all their dogs and give them thorough health checks by veterinarians before placing them for adoption.

* Most shelters charge adoption fees to help recover some of the cost of boarding, feeding, and caring for the dog, but these fees are much less than the cost of buying a dog from a store or breeder.

Animal shelters have many different purebred and mixed breed dogs to choose from.

Dog Euthanasia

✦ If your dog's quality of life deteriorates signficantly, either as the result of illness or simply old age, you may feel that your pet is in such distress or pain that the best course of action is to put the dog to sleep—euthanasia. This is a difficult decision, so take time to discuss it with your veterinarian until you are satisfied that it is the kindest option.

✦ Dogs are usually euthanized by barbiturate overdose, administered as an injection that rapidly sends the dog into unconsciousness before death. It is a painless procedure, and some veterinarians will euthanize the dog in the pet's home environment, rather than at the surgery.

✦ Consult the veterinarian about what to do with your pet's remains. If you wish, most will arrange to have the dog cremated, and you can request to retain the dog's ashes. Another option is to bury the dog in a pet cemetery.

Mementos, such as a portrait, can help owners while they grieve for lost pets.

Pet cemeteries offer plots, headstones, and monuments, just as human cemeteries do.

Continued from page 62

How Smart Is Your Dog?

45 Siberian Husky
   Bichon Frise
   English Toy Spaniel

46 Tibetan Spaniel
   English Foxhound
   Otterhound
   American Foxhound
   Greyhound
   Wire-haired Pointing Griffon

47 West Highland White Terrier
   Scottish Deerhound

48 Boxer
   Great Dane

49 Dachshund
   Stafforshire Bull Terrier

50 Alaskan Malamute

51 Whippet
   Shar-Pei
   Wire Fox Terrier

52 Rhodesian Ridgeback

53 Ibizan Hound
   Welsh Terrier
   Irish Terrier

54 Boston Terrier
   Akita

55 Skye Terrier

56 Norfolk Terrier
   Sealyham Terrier

57 Pug

58 French Bulldog

59 Brussels Griffon
   Maltese

60 Italian Greyhound

Continued on page 65

64

What's the use of a collar tag when I can't read? I'm only number 71 on the list of smart dogs, you know.

Basset Hound

HOW MANY DOG BREEDS ARE THERE?

It is estimated that there are over 400 different dog breeds, excluding all the new "designer" mixed-breed dogs that are being created.

Continued from page 64

How Smart Is Your Dog?

MICROCHIPPING

❋ A collar with a tag on it is a great way of identifying your pet, but collars sometimes get lost or can easily be removed. A microchip is a more effective way of permanently linking pets to their owners, increasing the chances of their being reunited if the animal is lost, stolen, or strays.

❋ A microchip is a rice-sized electronic circuit chip that is painlessly injected under the animal's skin. The microchip does not move under the skin or get lost, and holds a unique identification code that can be read by a monitor.

❋ Once an animal has been microchipped, the chip's unique code is logged onto a national database with the dog owner's details.

Choosing the Right Breed

Once you have decided that you are ready for a dog, you need to make sure that you choose the right breed of dog for your lifestyle and family. Here are some tips on what you should consider when making your decision.

CHARACTERISTICS

+ Each breed of dog has its own distinct characteristics (looks, size, character, and temperament), so it is essential to get as much information as possible about the breeds you are interested in to enable you to select the right dog to meet your requirements.

+ An advantage of a purebred over a crossbred is that there should be no real surprises. It is possible to predict, with fair accuracy, the ultimate size and appearance of the dog, the amount of coat care and exercise that it will require, what health issues may arise, its response to training, and its personality. This predictability should make it easy for anyone to select a puppy or adult dog that will enhance their life, and that they will come to love and value.

+ Be aware that looks can be deceiving. Some big, macho-looking dogs are great big softies, and some small breeds are famed for ill-humor.

There are hundreds of purebreds to choose from, plus a multitude of crossbreeds and mixed breeds—do your research before making a choice.

Black Great Dane

French Bulldog

Beauceron crossbreed

Bernese Mountain Dog puppy

BRED FOR A JOB

* There are over 400 different breeds of dogs that are recognized by the major international kennel clubs, and all of these dogs are grouped according to the jobs that they were bred to do. When you choose a purebred dog, then all the dogs of that breed will have the same job, but if you choose a mixed breed dog, then the dog may have been bred for more than one type of job. It is very important that you understand what job or jobs your dog was bred for.

* Some dogs, like English Springer Spaniels and Border Collies, have very high working instincts. They are intelligent breeds and need mental stimulation to ensure that they do not become bored and destructive in the home.

* If you do not want to work your dogs, you can enroll them in different types of classes and workshops to keep their active minds busy and working instincts intact. There are many classes in agility, flyball, and obedience.

GROOMING NEEDS

✦ Dog grooming is an important thing to consider, because some dogs need to be brushed daily, while others can get by with a few times a month.

✦ Problems arise when a prospective owner makes a choice based primarily on a puppy's appearance— be aware that fluffy puppies usually grow into dogs needing a great deal of coat care.

✦ Longer haired dogs are also more likely to shed if anyone in the family has allergy issues.

Border Collie

Harlequin Great Dane

Cane Corso

Chihuahua

Azalea

HARMFUL PLANTS

There are around 400 plants that are poisonous to dogs, some of which can even be fatal. The most common plants you should avoid are:

❀ *Aloe*

❀ *Azalea*

❀ *Baby's breath*

❀ *Begonia*

❀ *Buttercup*

❀ *Carnation*

❀ *Castor bean*

❀ *Common ivy*

❀ *Daffodil*

❀ *Dahlia*

❀ *Daisy*

❀ *All types of peace lily*

❀ *All types of common lily*

❀ *Oleander*

❀ *Tulip bulbs*

Tulip bulb

NON-SPORTING BREEDS

☆ This term describes a collection of dissimilar breeds that no longer have a clearly designated purpose, other than that of human companion.

☆ This is the group of breeds from which many pet dogs are selected. Popular non-sporting breeds include the Poodle, Dalmatian, Chow Chow, and Lhasa Apso.

☆ Non-sporting breeds may well have performed some task in the past, such as the Dalmatian, a former carriage dog that used to trot alongside aristocrats' carriages for guarding and decoration purposes. In the main, however, they are now the dogs whose sole purpose in life is to be a companion to their owners.

The Chow Chow is an ancient Chinese breed with distinctive facial features, a huge personality—and a large, blue tongue.

DOG BREATH

"Dog breath" is not a normal canine phenomenon. In the majority of cases, it is caused by dirty teeth and gums. Dogs' teeth benefit from brushing, just as ours do.

Speech bubble: I've got him beat on hairstyle, for sure, but I need to work on my teeth if I'm going to win the next ugliest dog contest.

Boxer crossbreed

Chinese Crested Dog

World's Ugliest Dog

+ There are many ugly dog competitions, but the annual Sonoma-Marin Fair in Petaluma, California, hosts the trademarked World's Ugliest Dog Contest. Dogs from around the world can enter.

+ Chinese Crested Dogs seem to excel in ugly dog contests. Chi Chi, a Chinese Crested from Palm Springs, California, won the title a record total of eight times. Chi Chi's grandson, Rascal, holds the record for winning the most titles from different ugly dog contests.

+ The 2009 award went to Pabst, a Boxer crossbreed from Citrus Heights, California.

ECLECTIC TRAINING METHOD

∗ Different dog training methods have been developed to achieve a variety of different goals. Methods include obedience training, working dog training, guide dog training, training for shows, competition training, and good citizen training.

∗ The eclectic training method combines different techniques, with an emphasis on whichever are most suitable for the purpose of the training and for the characteristics of the individual dog.

Choose a training method that suits your dog's character.

Dog Communication

Dog communication pertains to body movements and sounds employed by dogs to convey signals to other dogs and animals, including humans. It is important to observe and interrelate all of the dog's signals, because the same signal can have several different meanings. Understanding dog communication is of the utmost importance, especially when the dog is going to live around children.

TAIL

+ Alert: Tail and ears are held high.
+ Afraid: Tail is tucked between the legs.
+ Defensive: Fur on the tail stands on end.
+ Curious: Slight, slow wags of the tail and laidback ears.
+ Happy or excited: Tail wags rapidly.
+ Submissive: Tail wags and hips are pulled to the side.

FEET

+ Excited: Stamping the left and right forefeet while the hind legs remain still shows excitement, or a need for attention.

EYES AND BROWS

+ Interested: A raised eyebrow.
+ Confused or mildly angry: Lowered brows. One eyebrow raised may also suggest confusion.
+ Affection: Eyes narrowed to slits may signify affection for someone the dog is looking at.
+ Leave alone: Half-moon eyes means the dog wants to be left alone.

A fearful puppy tucks its tail between its legs, and lowers the front half of its body in a submissive gesture.

HEAD

+ Interested: Leaning the head to the right or left sometimes indicates interest in a newly heard sound that the dog is trying to understand.

EARS

+ Alert or listening: Ears are pricked.
+ Pleased, submissive, or about to attack: Ears held back against the head.

MOUTH

+ Sleepy or confused: A dog might yawn or lick its mouth when it is sleepy or wants to be left alone. However, this can also indicate that the dog is confused or stressed.
+ Happy or playful: Panting, either with relaxed lips that cover the teeth or with the mouth open.
+ Aggressive: A snarl with retracted lips and bared teeth. A vicious snarl showing all the teeth is a warning that the dog will attack if approached.

Pricked ears, relaxed mouth, and tilted head indicate interest.

VOCALIZATION

* Playful or excited: Short, sharp barks, or a whimper accompanied by licking, jumping, and barking.

* Stressed: A high-pitched, rhythmic bark that tends to soar in pitch as the dog becomes more disturbed.

* Threatened: A soft, low-pitched growl can mean that the dog is threatened and may attack. Growls should be observed carefully, because they can be a warning or threat. Conversely, a powerful growl with bared teeth can also be an invitation to play. Be very careful and exercise prudence when a dog growls.

* Anxiety or communication: Howling may be a sign of separation anxiety, such as when the dog's owner is away, or it may be an attempt to communicate with other dogs over a long distance. Dogs howl when they hear sirens or other loud noises, as a response to what they interpret as another howl.

* Wants attention: A high-pitched whine, produced through the nose with the mouth shut.

* Pain: A whimper or yelp. A whimper is lower in volume, softer, and higher pitched than a bark.

According to superstition, a howling dog portends sickness, death, or bad luck.

Conformation Shows

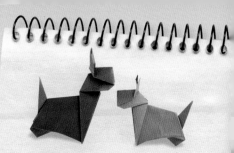

+ Sometimes referred to as breed shows, these are a kind of dog show in which judges evaluate purebred dogs for how well the dogs conform to the breed type—the characteristics that are typical of a breed. Breed type is outlined in a written breed standard for each breed.

+ Judges use their eyes and hands to analyze all the points of an individual dog, and then mentally compare that dog to the ideal for its breed (the standard). Dogs are judged against the ideal, not against each other. This requires a deep understanding of the breed's correct structure, and how that structure enabled the dog to fulfill the purpose for which it was historically intended.

+ The goal of conformation shows is to identify outstanding breeding stock.

BREED STANDARDS

❋ A breed standard is a written description of what a particular breed should look like and how it should behave, including ideal height and/or weight, desirable colors, movement, temperament, and so on. Breed standards are written for each breed by groups of hobbyists, called breed clubs. Details and definitions within breed standards may vary from breed club to breed club, and from country to country.

❋ Dogs always reflect the society in which they are bred, and the outlook on a standard in each country can change from time to time. If the changes become too great, a new breed arrives on the scene. A good example is the standard for the Cocker Spaniel, which eventually divided into two standards—the American and English versions.

EARLY SHOWS

One of the earliest recorded conformation dog shows was held in Newcastle-upon-Tyne, England, in 1859. Only Pointers and Setters competed, although other breeds were also shown. In 1863, the self-proclaimed "First Great International Dog Show" took place in Paris, with up to 2,000 dogs involved.

A Great Dane demonstrates its movement at a dog show in Kiev, Ukraine.

Playing and exercising with your dog is beneficial to both of you.

All dogs are happier if they have a purpose, but especially breeds such as the Newfoundland that were specifically bred for working.

MEETING YOUR DOG'S NEEDS

A dog needs a lot of care and commitment. It is not enough just to feed the dog once a day. Exercise and play are important, as is giving your dog something to do.

★ **Play**—One of the simplest things you can do to ensure that your dog lives a long, happy, and healthy life is to play with your pet. Take the dog outside and throw a ball or stick around. You will be doing yourself a favor by being active, but you will also be showing your dog that you care about it and enjoy spending time with it.

★ **Exercise**—Aside from playing with the dog, you should make sure that you exercise your dog regularly on lengthy walks. That does not mean taking your dog for a long hike, but do take at least 30 minutes daily walking your dog around. This will help keep the dog fit and prevent obesity and other diseases that arise as a complication of obesity.

★ **Obedience training**— Training your dog will make your life so much easier in the long run, plus it will help the dog be better socialized, both at home and out in public. It will be much easier to take the dog on a run if you are not worried about your pet disobeying your commands. Although you can train the

dog yourself, a great benefit from attending obedience classes is that you will have expert advice on hand.

★ **Jobs for dogs**—Dogs like having a purpose, just as humans do. There are many different ways of approaching this, from giving the dog a purpose in the home to training the dog to help out somewhere you volunteer. There are many organizations that use dogs therapeutically.

Commercial Dog Foods

Commercial dog foods are available in three main forms: canned, semi-moist, and dry. Many are complete diets, containing all the essential nutrients in the correct amounts. Others are intended to be mixed—for example, canned food with dry food.

A premium dog food will be specially formulated to meet a dog's nutritional and digestive needs at various stages in its life.

The cost element of feeding a dog should play a role in your choice of breed. Large breeds and working dogs cost considerably more to maintain, in food terms, than smaller ones.

Provided the dog receives a balanced diet, there is no reason why you should not mix different types of dog food—for example, dry food with a small amount of canned food added to make it more appealing.

Semi-moist meat

Canned meat

Dog biscuits

Complete dried food

Fresh meat

Dog biscuits

Chew sticks

Vitamin treats

Rawhide chew

Puppy mixer meal

CANNED FOOD

✦ Canned food comes in several varieties, ranging in quality as well as price. It consists of about 75 percent water, mixed with assorted meat, fish, and cereal products. Canned food is easy to prepare and dogs love it. However, canned food contains low-energy nutrients, which means that you need to give the dog a big serving in order to provide your pet with the required energy.

✦ If you have a large dog that requires large portions, canned food becomes impractical and expensive. To solve this problem, consider mixing canned food with dried food. The mixture will provide more energy for the dog, and will also add volume to the food, thereby saving money.

✦ There is another kind of canned food that contains only meat, hence called "all-meat canned food." On its own, it does not provide the dog with the proper amount of energy that its body needs, so it should also be mixed with dried or even semi-moist food.

SEMI-MOIST FOOD

✦ This high-concentration food contains only 15–30 percent water content, and provides more energy for the dog in less volume than canned food. The ingredients consist of meat, cereals, vegetables, sugar, and fats. Semi-moist food is tasty and easy for the dog to digest. It comes in a wide variety, does not need to be refrigerated, and many owners find it to be a convenient way to feed their dogs.

✦ Semi-moist food is expensive. It may also be loaded with sugar and corn syrup, which should not be given to dogs with diabetes. In addition, this food can contain colorings and artificial flavors. You may prefer to give your dog this type of food only occasionally, rather than as the main source of diet.

DRY FOOD

✱ Dry food, also known as kibble, contains about 10 percent water, providing high energy value to the dog. It is the least expensive of all the dog foods, can be stored in bulk quantities, and does not need to be refrigerated. This is why most pet owners prefer this type of food, and consider it to be the most economical way to feed their pets.

✱ Commercially prepared dried food tends to contain mostly cereal, so it is limited in terms of meeting a dog's protein requirements. Consider mixing dry food with canned food to give your dog a well-balanced diet, or choose a brand that contains meat as its main ingredient.

Good-quality commercial foods are both nutritious and tasty.

Sled Dog Racing

+ Sled dogs were once an important means of communication and transportation in areas such as Alaska, but nowadays these needs are met by aircraft, snowmobiles, cars, and telecommunications. This has led to a dramatic decrease in the use of sled dogs, with the result that they are now mainly just recreational.

+ Sled dog racing is a popular winter dog sport that involves the timed competition of teams of sled dogs. The dogs pull a sled, with the driver or musher standing on the runners of the sled. The team completing the marked course in the quickest time is judged the winner.

TAIL DOCKING AND EAR CROPPING

✽ Docking and cropping refer to the removal of part of the dog's tail or ears, respectively. Although sometimes performed as a medical necessity because of injury, they are usually elective surgeries.

✽ Originally, these practices were done to prevent injury to working dogs—a hunting dog's wagging tail can easily get caught and injured if the animal is working in an area with brambles, for example. However, the animal rights community's campaigns against docking and cropping contend that both practices are frivolous, painful, and unnecessary, and therefore cruel.

✽ The ongoing debate about the issue of elective surgeries for dogs has resulted in a ban on tail docking and ear cropping in Britain, Australia, and parts of Europe. Both are still allowed in the United States, Canada, and some other countries, but animal rights organizations in these countries continue to campaign against the practices.

A dog sled team competing in a race in Ashton, Idaho.

Shelter dogs make wonderful family pets if placed in the right home.

SHELTER DOG QUESTIONNAIRE

When getting a new dog from an animal shelter, you will probably be asked to fill out a pre-screening questionnaire. Although it may seem like a lot of work, these are many of the same things you would go through with a reputable professional breeder. Just remember that this system is in place to help ensure that the right dog goes with the right family.

THEY MAY ASK YOU

1) Have you ever owned a dog before?
2) Do you currently have other pets or children in the home?
3) Do you have a fenced yard or garden for the dog to play in?
4) Can you supply references?
5) Are you willing to have a home visit by a member of shelter staff to assess the situation?

YOU MAY ASK THEM

1) What vaccinations has the dog had?
2) What do you know about the dog's history?
3) Has the dog shown any behavioral problems or signs of aggression?
4) What information can you provide about the breed?
5) Do you offer training services?

🐕 WORLD'S OLDEST DOG

★ The oldest ever dog was Bluey, a working Australian Cattle Dog in Rochester, Australia. Bluey died in 1939 at 29 years of age—or about 203 in human years.

★ Max, a terrier mix from New Iberia, Louisiana, is the oldest living dog at 26 years of age—or 182 in human years.

Australian Cattle Dogs typically reach 10–13 years of age.

Pastoral Dogs

Pastoral dogs are those that have been bred to work with livestock. Although dogs are predatory animals, they possess many skills and abilities that make them naturally good at looking after other animals. Certain breeds are noted for having strong predatory instincts and aggression, but without the need to follow through and kill the animals they are protecting. Pastoral dogs do two main jobs: herding and guarding livestock.

HERDING BREEDS

+ Sheepdogs are the most well known of the herders. They are trained to use their natural predatory behaviors to make the animals under their care move in the direction that their handler (shepherd) requires. Herding dogs do this by nipping at the animals' heels, staring them down, or running behind them.

+ Various techniques and different breeds of dog are used for herding, and some are more effective than others with different types of animals. Sheep, cattle, and goats are commonly herded, but poultry also respond to dogs.

+ A more specialized type of herding dog is the drover. These do not move animals in the field, but instead drive them to market or across larger areas. They use the same methods as other herding dogs.

A Border Collie herding sheep by running behind them.

A shepherd moves his stock between pastures with the help of a drover dog.

GUARDIAN BREEDS

✳ Livestock guardian dogs do not move the animals, but instead protect them from predators. Guardian dogs may walk among the animals, or patrol around them, using their senses of smell, hearing, and sight to alert them to possible threats.

✳ If a guardian dog perceives a threat, it may attack the predator on its own or as part of a pack. More commonly, however, guardian dogs use threatening behavior, such as barking and growling, to drive the threat away.

✳ Guardian dogs are particularly useful in areas where the predators are endangered species that cannot be killed by the farmers. Farmers, not wanting to lose their stock, will use a pack of up to five dogs to guard their livestock.

✳ The training of guardian dogs is mostly social. They must be raised with the animals that they will be protecting, so that they do not view them as a prey animal. This process must happen early in the dog's life, usually at 3–16 weeks old. Beyond this time, they can only protect the type of animal they have been trained to guard—a guardian dog of sheep would not have the same protective instincts toward cattle, for example.

POPULAR PASTORAL BREEDS

• Border Collie
• Old English Sheepdog
• Rough Collie
• Briard
• Estrela Mountain Dog
• Finnish Lapphund
• Hungarian Puli
• Komondor
• Samoyed

A Maremma Sheepdog watching for potential threats as it guards a flock of sheep. The Maremma's large, solid build and fiercely protective instincts make it an ideal guardian dog.

A bitch will be receptive and invite a male to mate when she is in heat—that is, during the estrus part of her reproductive cycle.

The Reproductive Cycle

Every six months or so (in some breeds only once a year), a female dog comes into heat, which is when she becomes fertile and attractive to male dogs. The female dog's reproductive cycle contains four parts: anestrus, proestrus, estrus, and metestrus.

✤ Anestrus is the quiet time between heats, lasting three to five months or longer.

✤ Proestrus is the onset of the heat and accompanying bloody discharge. The follicles containing the eggs mature over approximately nine days. Most females refuse mating at this time. Though flirtatious when it comes to actual mating, they discourage males by baring teeth, growling, snapping, and sitting down. Some eager matrons, however, cooperate at any time. Fertilization cannot occur during proestrus.

✤ During estrus, the female accepts—in fact, invites— mating with a male. The bleeding often decreases and becomes pale in color. The receptive period of four days to a week is when ovulation takes place. Some females become quite obvious in drawing attention to themselves. They rub against fences separating them from the male, encouraging his advances. They eagerly move (flag) their tails to the side or curl them completely over their backs. Timeliness can be checked by rubbing the female just above the root

of her tail. If she flags, she is approaching ovulation. Toward the end of the season, the discharge becomes brownish.

✤ Metestrus is the stage that readies the uterus for pregnancy. If fertilization does not occur, this stage soon reverts to anestrus. A prolonged metestrus (called a false pregnancy) is common. If pregnancy exists, metestrus continues until delivery.

MAVERICK AND MISS MURPHY

☆ *Maverick and Miss Murphy are twin brother and sister Australian Cattle Dog crossbreeds living in Ormond Beach, Florida. Both dogs have a cleft palate that makes each dog look as if it has two noses.*

☆ *Owner Nucci Cento has written a children's book entitled* Maverick and Miss Murphy at Rascal's Rescue Ranch, *published in 2009. Planned as the first in a series, the aim of the book is to encourage children to accept the differences in one another.*

ARTHRITIS

+ Arthritis affects 1 in every 5 dogs. Arthritis occurs in dogs for several reasons, including a genetic predisposition, obesity, poor nutrition, trauma, and just old age.

+ The most common manifestation of the disease is as osteoarthritis, where the cartilage and bone degenerate.

+ Treatment is similar to that for humans with arthritis, including dietary changes, exercise, and anti-inflammatory medication. Dogs with arthritis must be kept slim, so that their joints have less weight to bear. Exercise needs to be regular. It is best to have one or two short walks every day, rather than one long walk on weekends. Swimming is a good form of exercise for dogs with arthritis, but not in extremely cold water.

A dog taking a walk on the beach with a little help from a pair of wheels.

The History of Dog Training

The goal of dog training is to establish a bond between the dog and other family members, and to enjoy the training process. Dog training methods have evolved throughout the years.

✦ In 1885, S.P. Hammond wrote in his book *Practical Training* that dogs should be praised and rewarded with meat whenever they accomplish something correctly.

✦ In 1898, Edward L. Thorndike published *Animal Intelligence*, in which he expounded a theory of learning based on stimulus and response, stating that animals learn faster with positive reinforcement.

✦ In 1903, Ivan Pavlov published his experiments on classical conditioning that showed that animals can be trained to have physical response to stimuli.

✦ In 1929, Dorothy Harrison Eustis established the Seeing Eye Foundation to train guide dogs for the blind.

✦ In 1938, B.F. Skinner started research in operant conditioning, which trains the dog's voluntary behavior by associating that behavior with a positive or negative consequence.

✦ Before World War I, dogs were trained using patience, understanding, and rewards. During the war, a large number of dogs were harshly and abruptly trained as service dogs. When World War II broke out in 1939, more young men were taught this harsh training method.

✦ In 1943, Marian and Keller Breland established the Animal Behavior Enterprise (ABE) that trained animals for shows. They pioneered the use of clicker training (where the dog learns to associate the sound of a clicker with desired behaviors) combined with operant conditioning, which they learned from B.F. Skinner.

✦ In 1978, Barbara Woodhouse published *No Bad Dogs*, one of the first bestsellers on basic dog training. The book promoted the proper use of chain collars and physical correction methods.

✦ The 1980s brought the concept of pack leadership, alleging that it is impossible to teach a dog anything unless you are the pack leader. "Dominance" was the prevailing word in dog training.

✦ In 1985, Karen Pryor published *Don't Shoot the Dog: The New Art of Teaching and Training*, in which she promoted clicker training. The method focuses on timing, positive reinforcement, and shaping behavior.

Using a food reward to train a dog.

The Shar-Pei is one of 14 ancient dog breeds.

The New Guinea Singing Dog is named after its native Papua New Guinea and the melodious sound of its howl.

ANCIENT BREEDS

✤ The New Guinea Singing Dog and the Australian Dingo have both been around for thousands of years. They are believed to be the last representatives of ancient primitive semi-domesticated dog breeds.

✤ Genetic research published in 2004 identified 14 breeds of dog that share a similar genetic fingerprint to wolves, making them the most ancient of the modern breeds. The 14 breeds are: Chow Chow, Pekingese, Shar-Pei (China); Akita Inu, Shiba Inu (Japan); Tibetan Terrier, Shih Tzu, Lhasa Apso (Tibet); Saluki (Egypt); Afghan Hound (Afghanistan); Samoyed, Siberian Husky (Siberia); Basenji (Congo); and Alaskan Malamute (America).

✤ The predominance of breeds associated with China, Japan, and Tibet supports a theory that dogs originated in Asia.

WHY DO DOGS SOMETIMES SCOOT ALONG ON THEIR REARS?

★ A dog scoots (drags its bottom across the floor) to relieve irritation. Intestinal worms are one possible cause for this discomfort. Look out for squirming segments of a live tapeworm, or the rice-like appearance of dried segments. If you think your pet has worms, consult a veterinarian, who will prescribe appropriate treatment.

★ Scooting could also indicate that the dog's anal sacs have become impacted or infected. Fecal material can remain on long-haired dogs, and this can cause a smelly and itchy mess that needs to be cut out of the hair prior to bathing.

★ You need to keep an eye on this area, especially when you bathe your dog. Make sure that you keep the hair clipped short and clean around the anus. (Your dog's groomer or veterinarian can take care of the job for you if you would rather leave this task to someone else.)

Puppies vs. Older Dogs

Once you have decided to enter into the exciting world of dog ownership, you need to decide whether you want a puppy or an older dog. While puppies are cute and cuddly, remember that they will not stay small for long, and there are many adult dogs that need a good home as well.

CHOOSING A PUPPY

+ Although adorable, puppies are a lot of work. Most puppies will still need housetraining and behavior training when you get them.

+ Puppies may try to chew everything, from the television remote to your favorite pair of shoes.

+ Puppies require a lot of time and attention to help them grow into healthy, well-behaved dogs.

+ Puppies have not yet grown into their personalities, so it is harder to predict accurately how your pup might act as it grows into adolescence and adulthood.

+ Puppies have not grown into their bodies yet, so you may end up being surprised by how big or small your pup ends up when fully grown.

+ Puppies need more trips to the veterinarian than most adult dogs, because pups will not have had all their vaccinations yet.

Puppies require a series of vaccinations before they can go outside.

ADJUSTMENT TIME

Whether or not you choose to get a puppy or an older dog, remember that your new pet will need a period of adjustment to get used to you, other family members, and their new home. This is a stressful time for a dog of any age, so if your dog has accidents indoors or chews on something it should not (particularly an adult dog), do not assume that the dog is not housetrained—it is just trying to get the lay of the land.

CHOOSING AN ADULT DOG

* Adult dogs still require love and attention, but they are not as needy as young puppies.

* Many older dogs will already be housetrained and know basic behavioral commands, like "Sit" and "Stay."

* Adult dogs have already gone through the chewing stage and may be calmer in temperament.

* Before adopting an adult dog, you have the chance to watch how they behave, so you can easily see their good and bad behavioral traits and what you may need to work with—unknown factors with a puppy.

* Adult dogs are already fully grown, so you know exactly what size of dog you are getting and exactly what the dog looks like.

Choosing an adult dog allows you to assess their temperament before you make a final decision.

WHAT HAPPENS DURING NEUTER SURGERY?

Neutering involves the removal of the reproductive organs. In female dogs, the operation is referred to as spaying. Spaying is major abdominal surgery, while neutering a dog is a simpler procedure.

✦ During neuter surgery, the veterinarian sedates the dog and puts it under general anesthesia. For male dogs, the surgeon makes a small incision in the front (toward the dog's head) of the scrotum. Each testicle is removed and the blood supply and vas deferens (spermatic cord) are tied off. For female dogs, the surgeon makes a small incision in the dog's belly area and removes the ovaries, fallopian tubes, and uterus. In both cases, the veterinarian finishes the procedure by closing the incision with surgical glue or sutures.

✦ Most dogs stay in the veterinarian's surgery overnight, although some can go home the same day. To ensure a speedy recovery after neuter surgery, you must keep the dog in a quiet place and restrict unnecessary activity. Try to prevent the dog from licking the incision excessively. Monitor food and water intake, according to the veterinarian's instructions.

Poster advertising a dog show in Mascoutah, Illinois, in 1901.

A FEW OF YOUR DOG'S FAVORITE THINGS

- Digging a hole.
- Swimming.
- Playing with other dogs.
- Chasing a ball or frisbee.
- Chewing a chew toy.
- Playing in the garden or yard.
- Riding in a car.
- Chasing birds and animals in the park.
- Playing tug-of-war.
- Going for a walk.

DOG FANCYING

🐾 By the mid-19th century, "dog fancying"—the selective breeding of dogs for particular features—had become very fashionable. Many of our current breeds came into being during that time. This was coupled with the rise of competitive dog shows, where various breeds were paraded and judged, with prizes being given to the winners in each category.

🐾 The original purpose of dog shows was to allow dog fanciers to compare their dogs with those of other breeders. As well as the competitive thrill of winning a prize, the shows gave dog enthusiasts the opportunity to find outstanding dogs for purchase, or to breed to their own dogs to incorporate additional desirable genes into the breeding program.

🐾 Governing bodies were created to regulate competitive dog shows. The Kennel Club was formed in Britain in 1873. It published a stud book of prize-winning pedigree dogs, and established breed group classifications and show rules. The American Kennel Club was established in 1884, with similar organizations soon following around the world.

Tough Training

Police dogs may face a wide range of challenges, so they must successfully complete a rigorous training regimen.

+ Police dogs may face loud noises, massive crowds, and objects being thrown at them; they may even be exposed to fire. They must cope with all of these without bolting or becoming scared, which is achieved by the incremental exposure to similar situations during their careful training.

+ Police dogs often face dangers together with their handler, so they may have to get used to wearing protective items. The shared danger helps to engender an incredibly close relationship between dog and handler.

+ The hard career of a police dog lasts for about six years. They are retired when they become too old, are injured, or bear or are nursing pups.

A Belgian Malinois Shepherd Dog being trained to scramble over high walls.

A Belgian Malinois Shepherd Dog carrying a weight in its mouth as it jumps a hurdle during police dog training.

Assistance Dogs

Assistance dogs are trained to assist people who have special needs. This includes guide dogs for the blind, hearing dogs for the hearing impaired, and seizure dogs for epileptics.

The working/obedience intelligence of Golden and Labrador Retrievers makes them ideal breeds for training as guide dogs for the blind.

A Labrador Retriever assistance dog and its proud owner.

GUIDE DOGS

+ Guide dogs are trained to help people with a visual impairment to navigate, primarily outside of the home. The dogs wear a special harness that is designed to make it easy for the dog to signal to the handler, and they will do so to indicate that there is an obstacle in the way, such as a curb to step down, and to move both themselves and the handler around a stationary or moving object.

+ Training will be conducted in many different areas, not just inside the home, and will include road safety. This is because when the dog is working, it may face large crowds, noisy situations, and other severe distractions that could stop it from safely performing its job, putting the handler in danger.

+ Most professionally trained working dogs will take commands and cues from only a single handler, but guide dogs are trained to listen to commands from more than one person. This is necessary to enable the dog to move from its trainer to the visually impaired person whom the dog will be assisting.

HEARING DOGS

+ During their training, hearing dogs are exposed to the same kinds of conditions as guide dogs, because they are also likely to face many distractions and complicated situations, requiring that their comprehensive training be both indoors and outdoors.

+ Hearing dogs are trained to alert their handler when certain noises occur, such as the ringing of a fire alarm, doorbell, or telephone, or when they hear traffic approaching that the handler may not have noticed. They may even be trained to fetch the handler when a baby is crying.

SEIZURE DOGS

* The training for seizure dogs is on a case by case basis, because the dogs need to be trained to meet the specific needs of the handler. They may be trained to move potentially dangerous objects away from the seizing person, or to stop a person who blanks out from walking into dangerous objects, or to fetch help for them. The help may come in the form of another person in the household, or the dog may press a medic alert device that dials out via a telephone.

* Seizure dogs are not trained to anticipate a handler's seizure, but may develop this skill over time. Those that do are able to warn the handler of a seizure before it happens, so that the handler can take medication to prevent the seizure or else get themselves into a safe situation to ride out the episode.

Hearing dogs need to be friendly, energetic, and eager to please— such as many of the toy breeds.

German Shepherd Dog Strongheart helps to rescue a damsel in distress in "The Silent Call," his first movie role in 1921.

Stroncheart

+ Strongheart was the canine star of several silent Hollywood movies in the 1920s, including *The Silent Call* (1921) and *White Fang* (1925).

+ Strongheart was a German Shepherd Dog that originally trained as a police dog in Germany. The dog's real name was Etzel von Oeringen.

+ The canine star died from the result of a tumor caused when he burned himself on a hot studio light during the making of a movie. However, Strongheart's numerous offspring have helped to continue his line to this day.

+ Strongheart was the first major canine Hollywood celebrity, and a huge box-office draw. The dog traveled the United States by train, making personal appearances and promoting his movies.

+ Strongheart Dog Food, first produced in 1927, is still manufactured today.

WHY DO DOGS EAT GRASS?

❀ Most dogs eat grass, and some dogs do it more than others. It is not known why they do so, but dogs have very flexible tastebuds and will eat, or at least try, whatever they can find.

❀ There is a good reason for their varied tastes. Early dogs survived by scavenging, and would eat whatever they could get their paws on. If meat was not an option, then plants and leaves would have to do. They simply could not pick and choose what to have for dinner, and dogs today have not become any fussier. They like just about everything.

❀ There is some evidence that dogs get cravings for certain foods, and it is possible that dogs occasionally get a hankering for greens. It is not as strange as it may sound—grass was part of their ancestors' daily diets.

❀ Dogs are omnivores, which means they eat both plants and meat. They do not need leafy nutrients any more, because most of today's dog foods are nutritionally complete. However, dogs' instincts still tell them that grass is good, so they eat it.

A Jack Russell Terrier puppy chews a stalk of grass.

DIGESTIVE OBSTRUCTION

Dogs with partial digestive obstructions have been known to eat huge amounts of grass to induce vomiting, apparently in an attempt to shift the obstruction. If grass-eating is accompanied by loss of appetite, weight loss, and diarrhea, consult a veternarian. Otherwise, the occasional eating of grass is not harmful.

Dog Parks

+ More and more designated parks are being built specifically for dogs. These dog parks are the most popular spots in towns and cities for owners to take their dogs.

+ The dog park is the one place where owners can let their dogs run off-leash (but it should always be under the careful supervision of the owners), and meet and play with other friendly canines. Many dog owners like going to the parks as well, because it gives them the chance to meet and chat with other dog owners.

+ The facilities offered at dog parks vary, but the parks are typically surrounded by a high fence and have a double-gated entry for security. Most provide benches (for humans), shade from the sun, and a water supply. There are also covered trash cans for the hygienic disposal of dog waste. Some dog parks even have a pond for the dogs to swim in, and a separate enclosure for small dogs.

+ Research shows that dog parks help to promote responsible dog ownership, and provide healthy exercise and socialization opportunities for dogs.

Trees provide essential shade in the dog park during hot weather.

DOGGY PHRASES
★ "Working like a dog." (very hard)
★ "Living a dog's life." (miserable)
★ "Dog tired." (very tired)
★ "Call the dogs off." (stop attacking)
★ "Sick as a dog." (very sick)
★ "In the doghouse." (out of favor)
★ "If you lie down with dogs, you'll get up with fleas." (suffer the consequences of foolish actions)

Dogs are happier and healthier if they get plenty of exercise and the chance to socialize.

Similar to dog parks, there are also dog beaches where dogs can swim, run, and play together off-leash.

TOY BREEDS

☆ The term "toy" is not a precise classification, but dogs traditionally referred to as toy breeds are usually the very smallest dogs.

☆ Toy breeds can be one of several dog types. Some are ancient lapdog types, while others are small versions of hunting dog, spitz, or terrier types, bred down in size for a particular kind of work or to create a pet of convenient size.

☆ Popular toy breeds include the Pomeranian, Maltese, Pug, and Chihuahua.

☆ Most toy breeds are splendid guards, keenly intelligent, energetic, affectionate if somewhat possessive—and courageous to the point of stupidity.

The Chihuahua is the smallest of the toy breeds—indeed, of any dog breeds.

The Pomeranian is a toy breed descended from much larger spitz-type dogs, bred down in size to create a lapdog.

The Three Behavior Drives

There are three drives that influence a dog's behavior, as outlined by renowned dog trainers Jack and Wendy Volhard.

❶ **Prey Drive**—This is highlighted by hunting and foraging behavior, and is exhibited by dogs that pursue anything that moves, sneak food, trail other animals, or pounce on toys.

A gundog retrieving a duck is an example of the prey drive.

A St. Bernard enjoying being groomed— a demonstration of the pack drive.

❷ **Pack Drive**—This demonstrates a dog's kinship with other dogs or with humans. It is exhibited by dogs that incessantly bark and whine when left alone, love playing and petting, like touching, and enjoy grooming.

This dog, hiding behind its owner's legs, displays the flight behavior of the defense drive.

❸ **Defense Drive**—This governs the dog's instincts for survival and self-preservation. This drive manifests in two forms: fight or flight. Fight behavior is a sign of a dog's self-confidence and defensiveness. It is exhibited by dogs that stand their ground, protect their territory, their family, and their belongings, and are ready to fight for them. The dog endures petting and grooming, but does not relish such activities. Flight behavior is another sign of defensiveness, and demonstrates a lack of self-confidence. It is exhibited by a dog that hides behind its master when confronted with new situations, is stressed with separation, is submissive and urinates when reprimanded, and may bite when trapped.

Temperament tests simulate a walk on-leash through a park, gauging the dog's reaction to various stimuli.

TEMPERAMENT TESTING

In 1977, Alfons Ertel founded the American Temperament Testing Society (ATTS) to provide uniform temperament tests for all breeds of dogs. The tests focus on shyness, stability, friendliness, and aggressiveness, as well as the instinct for protectiveness toward the handler and/or self-preservation. The data is cumulative, and of the nearly 29,000 dogs tested by the beginning of 2009, the average ATTS passing percentage for all breeds was 81.9%. The average score for mixed breeds was 85.4%.

EFFECTS OF THE THREE BEHAVIOR DRIVES

✤ Dogs are natural predators, and the obvious manifestations of predatory behavior should be redirected or arrested before adolescence. It is not wise to bring an adult dog with a well-developed prey drive into a home that has small children or other pets.

✤ A dog instinctively sets up its territorial boundaries around itself. Whenever someone perceived as a threat sets foot inside the dog's territorial boundary, it will elicit a fight or flight instinct. Keep in mind that most dogs will choose to fight first rather than run.

✤ A dog shows signs or warnings of its moods and feelings, and these convey signals for its potential behavior. A keen observation and understanding of these signs and warning signals would ensure a better and safer home environment for the canine pets and the family members.

Keep in mind that most dogs will fight rather than run, so watch out for warning signals.

Sniffer Dogs

A dog's sense of smell is far more acute than a human's. Through careful training, sniffer dogs are taught to recognize particular scents, and to alert their handler if they find them. Sniffer dogs are best known for their use in drug detection.

+ The dogs that are best suited to the role of sniffer dog not only have an excellent sense of smell, but are also very playful animals, because this helps with their training. They are often selected from animal rescue shelters, and are those animals that were given up because they were too playful for their owner to deal with.

+ Training usually involves a series of games, such as playing with a ball that is scented with the required odor or other substance that the dog will later be required to detect. Dogs are rewarded with praise and play, and this is why a strong drive to play makes a dog a good candidate for becoming a detection dog.

+ Sniffer dogs are trained never to touch or consume the object of their search, because this could be harmful.

POPULAR SNIFFER BREEDS
• Bloodhound
• English Springer Spaniel
• Labrador Retriever
• Beagle

A police officer demonstrates drug detection with his German Shepherd Dog at a fair in the Czech Republic.

JOBS FOR SNIFFER DOGS

Drug detection—The dogs may work in many environments, including airports and other forms of public transport. They may have to enter the homes of people suspected of drug involvement, as well as vehicles suspected of being used to carry drugs. The dogs' extensive training enables them to detect the particular smell they are trained for, even when attempts have been made to mask it by mixing the drugs with other strong smells, such as perfume.

Vineyard bug detection—Bugs are a particular problem for vineyard owners, because they can destroy an entire crop. Dogs can be trained to detect the bugs, allowing for their early treatment before damage becomes extensive.

Termite detection—Sniffer dogs are used by pest control companies to detect termite infestations. The dogs are far more accurate at picking up signs of an early infestation than any human inspection.

Sniffer dogs can be trained to detect bugs at vineyards, and termite infestations in buildings.

Sirius, the Dog Star.

The hottest days of summer were called "dog days" in ancient Greece and Rome.

"THE DOG DAYS OF SUMMER"

★ This phrase originates from ancient Greece and Rome, when the hottest, sultriest days of the summer were referred to as "dog days."

★ The ancient Greeks and Romans mistakenly believed that the heat was caused by Sirius, the Dog Star, which was the brightest star in the night sky.

★ The extreme heat could cause discomfort and miserable conditions, so this time of year was considered to be an evil period by many people in the ancient world.

Breeding Controversies

+ New breeds have been developed over the years for a variety of reasons, from making a dog that is better suited to a job (Bullmastiff or Airedale Terrier) to refining a breed to fit contemporary ideals of beauty (Afghan Hound).

+ When changes or refinements could be accomplished without sacrificing the breed's character, functionality, or soundness, clear improvements resulted. The new dog was usually healthier (benefits to the dog), and better able to perform a task (a benefit to the owner). In some cases, however, such as the English Bulldog and some toy breeds, breeders of the new versions accepted a certain degree of unsoundness as a fair return for other desired qualities.

+ Groups concerned with animal welfare have contended that the breed standards of kennel clubs and the judging standards at dog shows have led to breeders compromising the health of some purebreds as they try to meet those standards. Kennel clubs are now under increasing pressure to promote breed standards that focus on the dog's welfare, and that do not encourage breeders to exaggerate features that can be detrimental to a dog's health.

Mirror, mirror, on the wall, who is the fairest of them all? Why, it's me!

According to legend, the elegant Afghan Hound was one of the animals taken aboard Noah's Ark.

THE BROWN DOG AFFAIR

The Brown Dog Affair was a national cause célèbre in Edwardian England, polarizing opinions on animal vivisection. In 1903, physiologist William Bayliss was accused of infringing the 1876 Cruelty to Animals Act while performing the vivisection of a brown terrier dog in front of medical students at University College London. Bayliss, whose research on dogs led to the discovery of hormones, was outraged by the accusations and successfully sued for libel. Public opinion over vivisection was divided, and in 1906, anti-vivisectionists erected a bronze memorial statue of the dog in London's Battersea Park. The statue became a target of protest for animal researchers and medical students, leading to what became known as the Brown Dog Riots, and in 1910 the local council removed the statue to avoid more confrontations. A new memorial to the unnamed dog was erected in 1985.

The original Brown Dog statue in Battersea Park.

Most English Bulldogs have to give birth by Caesarean section.

CAESAREAN BIRTHS

Some breeds have been developed to emphasize certain physical traits beyond the point at which they can safely bear litters on their own. For example, an English Bulldog has wide shoulders and narrow hips, so the breed commonly requires artificial insemination and, later, a Caesarean section for giving birth.

BRINGING HOME A NEW PUPPY

Bringing home a new puppy is a very exciting time for the whole family and the dog. Follow these tips to make the transition to a new home a little easier for all involved.

✳ **Be the boss**—When you bring home a new puppy, be aware that you need to enforce expected behaviors from day one (this applies to older dogs as well). If you do not want the dog on the furniture or sleeping on your bed, then do not allow it from the moment the dog first comes in the door. You should be the one to go through the door first when entering or leaving a room. This will enforce to your dog that you are the pack leader.

✳ **Routine is key**—Adopt a predictable routine as quickly as possible. If you walk, feed, play, and take the dog out to relieve itself at the same time every day, your pet will feel more comfortable because it will know what to expect.

✳ **Get grooming**—Implementing good grooming habits while your puppy is still young will make things much easier for you and the dog as it gets older. Begin brushing, bathing, nail clipping, and checking the puppy's ears and teeth frequently, so that the dog will come to expect this behavior from you and hopefully will grow to enjoy it.

✳ **Socialize, socialize, socialize**—Socialization of a puppy is very important, so that it can get used to a wide variety of people and places. Try to take the puppy to as many places as you can, and introduce it to new people. The more a puppy is able to learn about the world, the less likely that it will be fearful of new places and things as an older dog.

Chocolate Labrador Retriever puppy.

Where's my mom?

Lots of socialization will help to prevent a puppy from growing up to be fearful of new things.

Children bonding with their new Belgian Malinois Shepherd Dog puppies by grooming them and playing with them. Take care to supervise young children when grooming.

PUPPY PARTIES

Puppy parties are held at dog training centers and veterinary practices to give puppies an opportunity to meet and communicate with other puppies and their owners, under supervision.

Puppies are very playful, and will benefit from canine as well as human company— not least for burning off excess energy.

Therapy Dogs

**The therapeutic benefits of contact with dogs is well known, and this has
led to the development of a number of visitation and contact programs
to provide companion dogs for those in need.**

Therapy dogs must be friendly, gentle, and patient, and enjoy physical contact and petting from lots of strangers.

THERAPY TRAINING

* All dogs and handlers that participate in these programs must be trained and screened to ensure that their temperament is right for the job.

* The dogs are trained to respond appropriately to being handled by multiple people, especially those who may (through no fault of their own) be a little rougher than most dogs are used to.

* When they successfully complete training, the dogs are also screened for health conditions that may adversely affect the patient, and are then certified as fit to visit.

* The dog's owner also has to be trained and certified, and any time given is normally on a voluntary basis. Annual recertification is common.

HELPING HOSPITAL PATIENTS

+ Patients are offered visits on a voluntary basis, during which time the hospital staff leave the patient, handler, and dog alone. Recovery times have been shown to be vastly improved in those patients who have access to this kind of program.

+ Therapy dogs are commonly used for longterm care, such as eating disorder treatment for young people, dementia care wards, oncology, and other areas of medicine where long admission times are common.

CARE HOME COMPANIONS

Residents of care homes may also benefit from visits by therapy dogs. Those who are limited in their mobility may have little or no other contact with animals, which may be particularly difficult for people who were dog owners before they entered the care home. This can lead to depression and other negative health issues, which the visits can help to overcome.

A therapy dog brings pleasure to an elderly care home patient.

Therapy dogs are often taught to perform small tricks to please their audience.

READING BUDDIES

Healthy children are included in therapy dog programs, such as the "reading buddies" program. In this, a volunteer dog that is trained to sit or lie down calmly for long periods of time spends time with a child, allowing the child to read to the dog and pet it. It has been found to be especially useful with children who are struggling or falling behind with their reading.

Children who are struggling with reading often become more relaxed and enjoy reading to a dog buddy.

The Stages of Puppyhood

Puppies are born with their eyes and ears closed, and spend around 90 percent of their time sleeping and most of the rest feeding. Once their eyes open (9–11 days after birth) and their ears (13–17 days), they quickly grow and develop.

A newborn Chihuahua.
At this stage, the puppy
is blind and deaf.

0 TO 7 WEEKS

This is a period when the environment opens up for a puppy. Its eyes and ears are excited to experience the sights and sounds of the world around it. This is a strong socialization period, as a bond grows between the littermates and mother. These bonds lead to a healthy, well-adjusted temperament. By day 10, however, the puppy should experience the touch of human hands and feel comfortable when being handled. This is a critical period for a puppy's physical and emotional growth. The mother passes on 65–75 percent of her temperament to her puppies. If she is calm, she will have a calming influence on a hyperactive puppy. The mother also passes natural antibiotics to the puppy through her milk during these weeks.

A French Bulldog mother with
her two 8-week-old puppies.

8 TO 12 WEEKS

Like a sponge, puppies at this stage absorb everything around them. They are curious and anxious to learn and play. At this age, puppy training can begin, the most important aspect of which is to create confidence. The training should be fun, not overly strict or aggressive. Negative experiences at this age can create impressions and behavior that can last the pup's lifetime. This is an impressionable stage, so it is important to have a positive attitude when working and playing with the puppy. The aim is to build a foundation for the puppy to develop positive patterns in its behavior.

3½ TO 4 MONTHS
Puppies at this age are losing their baby teeth. With any physical growth, there is a surge in hormones that affect the pup's behavior. If the puppy is hyperactive to begin with, it will become 30 percent more so during this period. If it is shy, it may become 30 percent more shy. During this period, you should adopt a consistent training schedule.

4 TO 5 MONTHS
At this age, many owners become mystified by the puppy's behavior. For example, the puppy may be toilet-trained one day, but urinate all over the floor the next. This is a common problem for many dog owners. Puppies are not being defiant at this stage, so never punish them. The problem is that they are getting a surge of hormones that confuse them. The best thing to do is take a few steps back, and then calmly reinforce the toilet training.

A Boston Terrier puppy tangled in holiday decorations—be patient when your puppy misbehaves.

5 TO 6½ MONTHS
Puppies go through a noticeable growth spurt during the fifth month. Spaying or neutering during this stage does not help—they will still go through a transitional phase.

6½ TO 7½ MONTHS
The puppy will settle down for a while.

A Boxer with her "teenage" puppies—hormones affect their behavior, just as with human adolescents.

7½ TO 9 MONTHS
This is the final hormonal surge for the puppy, when items around the house, such as remote controls, begin to disappear. This is a very challenging stage for owners, because a puppy's temperamental behavior will increase—a pup will be approximately 50 percent more aggressive, more shy, or more hyperactive. It is during this time that male dogs begin to lift their legs when urinating. Attention, not punishment, is what a pup needs during this time. All the training you have done may seem to have gone for naught, but try to avoid showing frustration, even if you think your pup should know better.

Making Your Own Dog Food

For most dog owners, commercial pet food is the most convenient and nutritionally complete method of feeding. However, some people choose to prepare their dog's food from scratch, so that they can control exactly what the dog eats. Always consult a veterinarian to check that you are feeding your pet a well-balanced and healthy diet. Also, be aware that certain ingredients can be harmful to dogs.

INGREDIENTS TO AVOID

- Alcohol
- Avocados
- Bacon
- Caffeine
- Chives
- Chocolate
- Corn
- Dairy products
- Garlic

Continued on page 107

Avocados are toxic to dogs, causing heart and breathing problems.

When making dog food, it is important to balance the dog's diet according to its age, size, activity level, and general health status.

A Beagle puppy enjoys a home-cooked meal.

Chocolate can be highly toxic to dogs, and at the very least is fattening.

Even a very small amount of grapes or raisins can cause renal failure in dogs.

CHOCOLATE WARNING

Most dogs love chocolate and may even beg for it. However, feeding chocolate to a dog can be very dangerous, and even fatal.

✿ Chocolate contains a chemical called theobromine. This has to be metabolized and cleared by the liver. In humans, this takes about two hours. In dogs, it takes 18 hours, and requires a lot of work by the liver. Toxic levels of theobromine can soon build up, especially if the liver is not functioning well.

✿ Some dogs are sensitive to theobromine, while others are not. Small dogs are most at risk. As little as 2 ounces per 2 pounds of body weight (50 g per 1 kg) can be lethal to pets that are sensitive to theobromine. This means that a small bar of chocolate could kill a Chihuahua.

✿ Cocoa is the most dangerous form of chocolate for dogs, followed by dark and then milk chocolate.

✿ Even if your dog is not sensitive to theobromine, chocolate is fattening and should only be given in very small amounts. Chocolate treats especially manufactured to be safe for dogs are widely available, but should still only be given in small quantities.

Continued from page 106

Ingredients to Avoid

- Grapes
- Macadamia nuts
- Nutmeg
- Onions
- Pork
- Raisins
- Salt
- Sesame
- Soy
- Sugar
- Sunflower oils
- Tomatoes
- Tuna
- Walnuts
- Xylitol (artificial sweetener found in diet products)
- Yeast, or any dough containing it

Nutmeg affects the dog's central nervous system, causing tremors, seizures, and even death.

Dog-proofing Your Home

Before bringing a new dog home, there are some things you need to check for to ensure that your pet will be safe and comfortable in your home and yard. All dogs, but especially puppies, are going to be extremely curious about their new surroundings. This is natural, but you need to make sure that the dog's environment is safe to explore. Dog-proofing your home is very much the same as baby-proofing your home, and is mostly just common sense. Here are some of the things you should check for.

+ Electrical cords are especially appealing to tiny, sharp puppy teeth, so make sure that they are out of reach of the dog.

+ Cords on draperies and blinds may be appealing to a new puppy and can pose a choking hazard, so put them out of reach.

+ Check with the veterinarian for any houseplants or garden plants that may be poisonous to your new dog.

+ Puppies love to chew, so check floors regularly to remove dangerous items. Things to watch out for include clothing with buttons, coins, marbles, small metal objects, jewelry, rubber bands, and paperclips. These items not only pose a choking hazard, but can also cause severe internal damage to the intestinal track.

+ If you have children, make sure that you keep their toys off the floor and out of the dog's reach, because many toys have small parts that the dog could swallow.

+ Just as you would for a small child, make sure that you keep all medications and personal toiletry items, like razor blades, placed well out of reach.

+ Cleaning products need to be stored where the dog cannot get to them.

+ Make sure that your garbage bins, particularly kitchen ones, have secure locking lids, because the smell of table scraps might be too much for the dog to resist.

+ If the dog will have access to a basement or garage, remember to dog-proof these areas as well. Dogs seem to love the smell and taste of anti-freeze, which is highly toxic. Fishing lines, lures, and hooks should also be stored away if the dog has access to these areas.

+ Check the garden where your dog will run and play. As well as making sure that the plants are not toxic to the dog, be sure to put all tools and other chewable items like garden hoses where the dog cannot get to them.

+ Keep your new dog where you can keep on eye on it. When you cannot do so, consider a crate or baby gates to keep the dog contained in a room that will be safe.

Puppies, such as this 8-week-old English Bulldog, love to chew, especially when teething.

These Jack Russell puppies are confined safely in a pet play pen.

A Labrador Retriever puppy chewing on a garden plant—check that there are no toxic plants in your yard.

A Dogue de Bordeaux puppy with collar and name tag.

LEATHER OR NYLON COLLARS?

It is advisable to use a round leather collar on puppies. Nylon collars tend to slip off their necks, and can tear at their hair. If you are going to use a nylon collar, make sure that it is at least 1 inch (2.5 cm) wide so that it will not grab at the dog's hair, especially if you have a long-haired puppy. Check that the collar is tight enough, so that the puppy cannot slip out of it. The collar is a proper fit if you can slip one or two fingers between the collar and the dog's neck. Some owners use a cat's collar for young pups. Some cat collars have a tiny bell, which comes in handy when you need to track the puppy's location quickly.

A leather collar is ideal for puppies.

World's Most Expensive Dog

✦ Yangtze River Number Two, a black Tibetan Mastiff measuring 31 inches (79 cm) in height, is the most expensive dog in the world. The dog was bought by a woman in China for 4 million yuan ($585,000).

✦ A Labrador named Lancelot Encore was the previous most expensive dog, bought by a family in Florida for $155,000. That price included the cost of cloning Lancelot Encore from their dead dog Lancelot.

The Tibetan Mastiff originated in central Asia, where it guarded flocks of sheep.

Large as an Ass

The Tibetan Mastiff is mentioned in the 13th-century chronicles of the explorer Marco Polo, who referred to them as being "as large as asses."

TIPS FOR THE DOG PARK

Considering how much fun taking your dog to a dog park can be, there are a few mistakes that some dog owners make when visiting these areas. People often forget to balance their dog's emotional needs while visiting the park.

❶ One of the biggest mistakes people make is to depend on the dog park for fulfilling all their dog's needs. In other words, because these areas are so enjoyable for the dogs, many owners start to neglect affection when they are away from the park. Somehow, they think that the one or two hours spent at the dog park negates the animal from needing other stimulation when away from the park. Doing so may cause your pet to become increasingly detached from you. This will cause behavior problems and distress at home.

❷ Another mistake dog owners sometimes make is not supervising their dogs closely enough when they are running loose in the park. The main issue is that of aggression and dominance over other dogs in the area. All of the animals will be excitable and full of high energy, so it is quite easy to misread your dog and miss the fact that it may be dominating another dog or puppy. While you may consider your dog's actions playful, sometimes they are quite the opposite, and your pet may be in the process of starting a fight.

❸ A third issue that you may want to consider when visiting the dog park is to include yourself in the activity. Many people let their dogs run free in the park, while sitting idly aside, watching all the fun. You must interact, watch your dog, and be careful of other more dominant dogs taking over. Place boundaries and keep your animal behaved. These are things that you cannot do when sitting on the bench reading a book. Think of your dog as a child—you would never take your child to the park and totally ignore his or her actions until it is time to go home.

A Siberian Husky displays dominant behavior over another dog at the park.

A well-behaved Doberman and Fox Terrier enjoy each other's companionship at the dog park.

Disney Dogs

+ *The Fox and the Hound* (1981) tells the story of a young hunting dog named Copper and an orphaned fox called Tod. Tod and Copper grow up as playmates and vow to be friends forever. The movie recounts their struggle to remain friends in adulthood, because foxes and hounds are natural enemies.

+ *Lady and the Tramp* (1955) tells the story of Lady, an American Cocker Spaniel that lives a pampered life with her owners, and Tramp, a streetwise stray mutt. The movie tells of their adventures and blossoming romance. A memorable moment in the film is when Lady and the Tramp eat a strand of spaghetti, starting at opposite ends and meeting in the middle.

+ *Disney's One Hundred and One Dalmatians* (1961) was based on a 1956 novel by Dodie Smith. The movie tells the story of two adult Dalmatians called Pongo and Perdita and their 15 kidnapped puppies. The evil Cruella De Vil wants to make a beautiful coat out of the stolen puppies' spotted fur. Pongo and Perdita eventually rescue their puppies—along with 84 more that Cruella has acquired. The film ends with all 101 Dalmatians living together in a large house in the country with Pongo and Perdita's owners.

HOLLYWOOD HOUNDS

Today, dogs are routinely featured in films, advertisements, and many other forms of entertainment, making it difficult to track resulting trends. The abundance of small dogs on the silver screen, such as the Chihuahua in *Legally Blonde* (2001) and the Brussels Griffon in *As Good As It Gets* (1997), combined with the bevy of jet-setting celebrities who tote their canine companions with them, appears to have fueled the popularity of the petite pooch.

Movies have fueled a trend for carrying small dogs, such as this Miniature Schnauzer puppy, as fashion accessories.

Registrations of Dalmatians doubled following the release of the Disney movie "101 Dalmatians."

Disney's clumsy but lovable Goofy was originally designed as a human character, which is why he walks upright and Mickey Mouse's pet dog Pluto does not.

Sierra Leone Le 20

GOOFY

HYDE

In the ultimate doggy date movie, Lady and the Tramp share a strand of spaghetti—and a kiss.

Kennel Clubs

Over 50 countries have their own registry for dog breeds, known as a kennel club, kennel council, or canine council. Most registries concern themselves with the classification and registration of dogs, the adoption and enforcement of uniform rules to regulate dog shows, and setting the breed standards by which recognized dog breeds must be judged. A kennel club that concerns itself with different dog breeds is sometimes referred to as an "all-breed club." Those that are limited to a single dog breed are known as a "breed club."

The largest dog registry is in India. The smallest registry is probably Guernsey, in the Channel Islands off the coast of France.

The Canadian Kennel Club (CKC) was founded in 1888.

The (British) Kennel Club (KC) was established in 1873, making it the oldest kennel club in the world.

The Australian National Kennel Council (ANKC) is an umbrella organization that incorporates Australia's eight canine organizations.

By far the greatest number of dogs is registered by the American Kennel Club (AKC) in the United States.

Many European, Central American, and South American national registries are members of the Fédération Cynologique Internationale (FCI), an international federation of kennel clubs.

MAJOR INTERNATIONAL KENNEL CLUBS

- American Kennel Club (United States)
- Australian National Kennel Council
- Canadian Kennel Club
- Kennel Club (United Kingdom)
- Kennel Club of India
- Kennel Union of Southern Africa
- Ente Nazionale della Cinofilia Italiana (Italy)
- Société Centrale (France)
- United Kennel Club (United States)
- Der United Kennel Clubs International (Germany)

SCOOP THAT POOP

Most urban and many other areas have laws regarding cleaning up after dogs. Dog feces can contain harmful organisms and be the cause of infection, so cleaning up after your dog is an important health matter as well as a social one.

CONDITIONING A DOG FOR CAR TRAVEL

Some dogs get nervous about traveling in a car, while others love it. Here are some tips for getting your dog conditioned for car travel. The following suggestions may help to alleviate the dog's fears, and can make the car travel experience fun for the both of you.

1) While the car is parked at home, open the back door and place the dog inside the car with a toy or treat. Let the dog get used to being inside the car with the engine off.

2) Now get inside the car and demonstrate that being inside the car can be a calming experience. Open the windows or switch on the radio.

3) Finally, switch on the engine and take the car for a short drive. Allow the dog to continue playing with its toys, which may distract the dog from the journey. After the short trip, make a fuss of the dog and take it for a walk or go for a play in a field. Repeat the same process, increasing the distance of the trip, until the dog gets to the point where it actually looks forward to going in the car.

Teach a dog that is nervous about car rides to associate them with something pleasant, such as a trip to the park.

Designer Dogs

+ The term "designer dog" became popular toward the end of the 20th century, when breeders began to cross purebred Poodles with other purebreds in order to obtain a dog with the Poodle's hypoallergenic coat in addition to desirable traits from the other breeds.

+ As the name suggests, a designer dog is one that has been bred by design from two selected breeds, as opposed to an accidental crossbreeding. Some breeders have attempted to create new breeds of dog by breeding designer crossbreeds to each other, documenting the puppies' ancestry, and setting a new breed standard.

+ The identifying mark of a designer dog is that the crossbreed is named with a portmanteau word made up of elements from the breed names of the two purebred parents, such as Puggle (Pug/Beagle cross) or Schnoodle (Schnauzer/Poodle cross).

+ Another characteristic of a designer dog is that it is bred to be a pet. Working dogs that are crossbred in order to create a dog more suited to a job are not given portmanteau names. They are usually referred to by type rather than breed—for example, Eurohound is the name given to a type of dog that has been crossbred from the Alaskan Husky and Pointer for sled dog racing.

This Schnoodle puppy is a cross between a Schnauzer and a Poodle.

SOME DESIGNER BREEDS

• Afador—Afghan Hound/Labrador Retriever

• Alusky—Alaskan Malamute/Siberian Husky

• Australian Collie—Australian Kelpie/Border Collie

• Bassador—Basset Hound/Labrador Retriever

• Beagador—Beagle/Labrador Retriever

• Boston Lab—Boston Terrier/Labrador Retriever

• Boxweiler—Boxer/Rottweiler

Continued on page 119

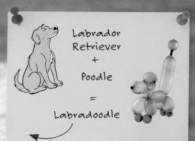

Labrador
Retriever
+
Poodle
=
Labradoodle

The Labradoodle
combines the
characteristics of
the ever-popular
Labrador Retriever
with a Poodle's
hypoallergenic coat.

DANCING DOGS

❁ Dancing with dogs has become a competitive sport involving a dog and handler performing a routine to music. There are two types: musical freestyle and heelwork to music.

❁ Musical freestyle demands that the dog demonstrate obedience talents and perform tricks. There is also more focus on the handler's dance moves.

❁ Heelwork to music relies on a dog's ability to stay in variations of the heel position while the handler moves in accordance to the music.

❁ The sport is popular in countries all over the world, and competition rules and styles vary, although most are based on a variety of technical and artistic points. Regardless of the style, all routines are done free of training aids or leashes (except in some beginner categories).

❁ Competition can be done as a single dog-and-handler team, as a pair of dogs and handlers, or as a full team of three or more dogs and their handlers. Generally, for competition, there is one dog to a person.

A dog jumps through its handler's arms during a freestyle musical routine, which involves the dog performing tricks.

LONGEST BREED NAME

☆ The longest English-language dog breed name belongs to the Nova Scotia Duck Tolling Retriever. The dog's job is to thrash about at the water's edge in order to attract the attention of wildfowl, a performance known as tolling. Most people shorten the dog's tongue-twisting name to Toller.

☆ The longest non-English-language breed name is Osterreichischer Kurzhaariger Pinscher, which is also known as the Austrian Short-haired Pointer.

A Nova Scotia Duck Tolling Retriever thrashes around in the water to attract wildfowl.

Continued from page 116

Some Designer Breeds

- Chestie—Chihuahua/
  West Highland White Terrier
- Chiweenie—Chihuahua/
  Dachshund
- Cockapoo—Cocker Spaniel/
  Poodle
- Dorgi—Dachshund/Corgi
- German Chusky—German
  Shepherd Dog/Husky/Chow Chow
- Jug or Jack-a-Pug—Jack Russell
  Terrier/Pug
- Labradoodle—Labrador
  Retriever/Poodle
- Malkie, Morkie, or Yorktese—
  Maltese/Yorkshire Terrier
- Mal-Shi or Malti-Tzu—Maltese/
  Shih-Tzu
- Pekeapoo—Pekingese/Poodle
- Peke-a-tese—Maltese/Pekingese
- Puggle—Pug/Beagle
- Schnoodle—Schnauzer/Poodle
- ShiChi—Shih Tzu/Chihuahua
- Shih Apso—Shih Tzu/
  Lhasa Apso
- Shih-poo—Shih Tzu/Poodle
- Sprocker—English Springer
  Spaniel/English Cocker Spaniel

The "hair of the dog" hangover cure is based on the premise that "like cures like."

"HAIR OF THE DOG THAT BIT YOU"

✳ This expression usually refers to drinking some alcohol to alleviate a hangover—in other words, use the cause of the illness as a remedy.

✳ The phrase is derived from a folklore cure for dog bites that required hair from the dog to be placed on the wound.

This puppy is a Maltese/
Shih Tzu cross, known as
a Mal-Shi or Malti-Tzu.

World's Tallest and Smallest Dogs

+ Irish Wolfhounds are the tallest breed of dog, but the tallest dog ever is George, a blue Great Dane from Tucson, Arizona. George measures 43 inches (109 cm) from shoulder to paw, and 87 inches (221 cm) from nose to tip of tail. He weighs 245 pounds (111 kg), sleeps in his own queen-sized bed, and eats around 110 pounds (50 kg) of food a month.

+ Chihuahuas are the smallest breed of dog, but the smallest dog ever recorded was a Yorkshire Terrier named Sylvia from Blackburn, England. When she died in 1945 at two years of age, Sylvia measured 2½ inches (6.3 cm) tall from shoulder to paw, and 3½ inches (8.9 cm) long from nose to tail tip. She weighed just 4 ounces (114 g).

+ The smallest living dog in terms of length is a smooth-coated Chihuahua named Heaven Sent Brandy from Largo, Florida, measuring 6 inches (15.2 cm) from nose to tail tip. She weighs 2 ounces (900 g).

+ The smallest living dog in terms of height is a long-coated Chihuahua named Boo Boo from Raceland, Kentucky, measuring 4 inches (10.1 cm) from shoulder to paw. She weighs 1½ pounds (680 g).

Great Danes and Chihuahuas regularly hold the record as the tallest and smallest living dogs in the world.

87 inches (221 cm)

43 inches (109 cm)

6 inches (15.2 cm)

4 inches (10.1 cm)

A bomb detection dog and its handler demonstrate their skills at the Windsor Castle Royal Tattoo, a military display, in England.

MILITARY DOGS

✤ Just as the police use detection dogs for civilian work, the military also use them. The only difference is the items that the dogs are trained to detect.

✤ Relying upon their sense of smell, dogs can help reduce the risk to soldiers and others working in areas where there are landmines. These explosive devices are normally hidden under the ground and are triggered when someone steps on or drives over them. They kill a great number of people, and finding the bombs is a dangerous undertaking.

✤ The dog's sensitive nose can detect the mine without the dog getting close enough to cause an explosion. After the dog alerts its handler to the location of the mine, the mine can then be safely detonated or removed and disarmed. Over the past few years, dogs have been used to help clear large areas of land that were riddled with mines. They work closely with a dedicated handler.

✤ Bomb detection dogs can also detect other types of explosives, such as trip wires and weapons hidden in civilian houses.

The Huntress
The Roman goddess Diana and her Greek counterpart Artemis were huntresses, often depicted with dogs in paintings and sculpture.

Statue of Diana from the Capitoline Museum in Rome, Italy.

TRAINING COLLARS

★ Owners need to learn how to use a leash properly before placing a training collar (also known as a chain collar or slip collar) on their puppy. Not knowing proper leash mechanics with a training collar can hurt the puppy. A puppy's bones are still soft and not fully formed, so you need to be careful about putting too much stress on the puppy's neck. The best time to work with a training collar is when you take the dog to puppy kindergarten classes.

★ A training collar should be shaped like a letter "P" when placed on the dog's neck, and it should be relaxed. A proper fit is when only four links come through the ring when the dog pulls. If more than four links come through the ring, the collar is too big and it can easily slip off. If fewer than four links come through, the collar is too tight. A training collar that is too tight makes the dog feel uncomfortable and does not release properly, and therefore defeats its purpose.

★ A training collar has been nicknamed the choke collar or chain choke because many owners use the training collar as a choking device. However, it is not a torture tool for training your dog. You work a training collar by listening to the sound of the links. When four or more links zip through the ring and become a tight fit around the dog's neck, then you know your puppy is pulling too far away from you. You need to release this hold by stepping toward the dog. This will relax the collar. Then maneuver the leash in the direction the dog should move.

★ A training collar should only be used during training sessions. Avoid accidents by taking the collar off when placing the puppy in the crate or in the house when you cannot keep a close eye on your pet.

Only use a chain collar during training classes, and make sure that it is a good fit for your dog.

Chain collars are effective training devices, as long as owners learn how to use them correctly.

Cultural Icon

Hachiko was a Japanese Akita owned by Professor Ueno, who worked at the University of Tokyo in Japan. Each day, Hachiko would walk for miles to meet the professor at the local train station when he returned from work. One day, the professor suffered a fatal stroke while at work and did not return. For many years after his master's death, Hachiko would escape from his new home to go to the station and wait for the professor. Hachiko's devotion to his owner impressed the people of Japan so much that he became a national symbol of family loyalty.

A bronze statue of Hachiko at Shibuya train station where he used to wait for his owner.

PET INSURANCE

There are numerous types of pet insurance policies, and it is important to choose a policy that meets your individual needs.

❋ Routine and wellness coverage is the least expensive. It covers routine preventive care items, such as teeth cleaning, spaying and neutering, vaccinations, and annual checkups.

❋ Major medical canine insurance covers emergency situations, such as an accident. It has a low premium, but a high deductible.

❋ Chronic condition insurance covers a variety of common chronic conditions, such as diabetes or osteoarthritis, as specified in the policy.

❋ Genetic condition coverage is one of the most expensive types. It covers genetic conditions, as specified in the policy.

❋ Comprehensive coverage is the best, but also the most expensive. It typically combines several of the other types of coverage, protecting your pet for a wide range of circumstances. Check the policy carefully to be sure what is covered.

Trips to the veterinarian can be expensive, so it may be wise to buy suitable pet insurance.

BRINGING HOME A NEW OLDER DOG

If you have decided to expand your family by getting an older dog instead of a puppy, remember that an adult dog will have some different needs from those of a puppy. Older dogs may have had previous owners that may not have treated them well, or they may have spent a good deal of their lives in a shelter. Bringing home a new dog should be a pleasant experience for both of you, so above all, remember to be patient.

★ **Show the dog around—** When you first get home with your new dog, take it outside to the area you want it to use as a toilet. Allow the dog to sniff around, and if it goes to the toilet, praise the dog profusely. If the dog does not go to the toilet initially, take it on a quick tour of the house and give it some water. After a few minutes, take the dog back outside and hopefully this time it will go. If not, just keep trying. If the dog is not toilet trained, the method is the same for adult dogs and puppies. Take it outside regularly and say something like "Toilet." If the dog relieves itself indoors, do not make a huge deal about it. Just clean up the mess, say "No," and then take the dog outside.

★ **Do your research—**Try to find out as much as possible about your new dog's past. If you are adopting from a shelter, they may not have a lot of information, but it never hurts to ask. Things that would be helpful to know are whether the dog has been toilet trained, had any behavior training, and what grooming habits it is used to.

★ **That's a good boy—**If your new dog has not had any behavior training, it is never too late to start. Just be patient with the dog, and offer lots of praise. You may also want to consider obedience classes, where a professional can help you achieve your desired results. Never hit the dog for doing something wrong; this will not make the dog learn any faster, and may make the dog fear you.

★ **Get grooming—**When it comes to grooming an older dog, you should start slowly if you do not know its previous grooming habits. For things like clipping nails, start by just holding the paw and touching the nails. When the dog is comfortable, start by clipping one nail at a time, and then increase this as the dog becomes more relaxed. Instead of jumping right in and giving the dog a bath, start by gently rubbing it with a warm, wet washcloth. As the dog learns that you are not trying to harm it, it will become a lot more comfortable with the new grooming practices.

Introduce grooming tasks slowly into your new dog's routine, to be sure that the dog is comfortable.

WHY DO DOGS PAW AND SCRATCH AT THINGS?

Most humans have a little bedtime ritual—toothbrushing, washing, and so on. For dogs, it is sometimes pawing the ground or the carpet before settling in. Dogs are creatures of habit, and every dog develops a slightly different set of night-time rituals. For the most part, the dog will follow the same rituals every time it lies down. As soon as a dog enters your home, it will scratch and dig just about anywhere—in the garden, on the carpet, even on tiled floors. The dog is not really trying to make a bed in all of these places; it just enjoys scratching and the feeling it has on its paws.

Dogs love to follow routines and rituals on their way to bed.

DOG PLAY PEN
Portable pens are available that can be used inside the home and outdoors. They are ideal if you need to confine your pet for any reason.

A Bernese Mountain Dog in a dog pen.

Michael Darling riding on the back of Nana, the dog who runs the children's nursery in the Peter Pan stories.

Dogs in Literature

In the 1939 movie adaptation of "The Wizard of Oz" starring Judy Garland, Toto is played by a Cairn Terrier.

✦ In the 1838 Charles Dickens novel *Oliver Twist*, Bill Sikes is a brutal villain who owns a white Bull Terrier named Bull's-eye. Treated viciously by Sikes, Bull's-eye displays "faults of temper in common with his owner."

✦ *The Wonderful Wizard of Oz*, published in 1900 as the first in a series of Oz books by L. Frank Baum, features a little black dog called Toto. Toto belongs to Dorothy Gale and accompanies her on her adventures in Oz.

✦ Jack London's *The Call of the Wild* (1903) is the story of a somewhat pampered St. Bernard/Scotch Shepherd Dog cross named Buck. After being stolen and sold as a sled dog, Buck's primordial instincts return and he succumbs to the call of the wild, leaving behind humans to run free with a pack of wolves.

✦ In J.M. Barrie's classic children's stories about Peter Pan, Nana is a Newfoundland dog that runs the nursery of the Darling family. Nana never speaks, but is an able and devoted carer of the children.

✦ The *Doctor Dolittle* series of books created by Hugh Lofting relate the adventures of a man who can talk to animals. In the first book, *The Story of Doctor Dolittle* published in 1920, the doctor's dog Jip uses its keen sense of smell to find and rescue a man stranded on an island.

✦ Fred Gipson's 1956 novel *Old Yeller* tells the story of a yellow Blackmouth Cur that turns up at a family farm and develops a strong bond with one of the sons, Travis. After several adventures, Old Yeller saves the family from a rabid wolf, but is bitten and infected in the process, forcing Travis to shoot the dog.

✦ *Where the Red Fern Grows*, a novel by Wilson Rawls published in 1961, tells the story of a boy called Billy who buys two Coonhounds and trains them to win a championship competition for treeing racoons.

✦ *Clifford the Big Red Dog*, published in 1963, was the first in a series of children's books created by Norman Bridwell. Clifford is as big as a house and accompanies his human friend Emily and his other dog friends on their adventures.

✦ In J.K. Rowling's *Harry Potter* books, the gamekeeper Hagrid has a large boarhound called Fang. Although Fang looks intimidating, Hagrid describes him as a coward. Fang is played by a Neapolitan Mastiff in the *Harry Potter* movies.

✦ John Grogan's *Marley & Me* (2005) chronicles Grogan's family life with a boisterous and somewhat neurotic yellow Labrador Retriever called Marley.

Vicious Bill Sikes and Bull's-eye in Charles Dickens's "Oliver Twist."

TRAVEL TIPS

❶ Do not feed the dog for about three hours before beginning a trip. You can offer the dog a snack while traveling, but do not provide a meal until you arrive at the destination.

❷ If the dog suffers from carsickness, discuss medication options with your veterinarian.

❸ If you do not have air conditioning in your vehicle, travel at night or during cooler times of the day.

❹ Keep the dog secured in the back of the car, either in a carrier or crate, or with a pet harness. This will prevent the dog from distracting you, and allows you to roll down the window without risk of the dog escaping.

❺ Make frequent rest stops so that the dog can relieve itself or have a drink of water.

❻ If the trip requires overnight accommodations, know ahead of time which hotels accept pets. Make reservations and let them know you will be bringing an animal. If you are camping, make certain the campsite allows pets.

❼ Make sure that the dog is wearing a collar with identification tags, or better still is microchipped, in case your pet gets lost. Take along a photograph of the dog in case you do get separated.

A pair of Cocker Spaniels, secured in the back of a car with pet harnesses.

A hotdog, a.k.a. wiener.

A Dachshund, a.k.a. wiener dog.

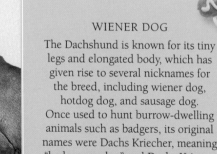

WIENER DOG

The Dachshund is known for its tiny legs and elongated body, which has given rise to several nicknames for the breed, including wiener dog, hotdog dog, and sausage dog. Once used to hunt burrow-dwelling animals such as badgers, its original names were Dachs Kriecher, meaning "badger crawler," and Dachs Krieger, meaning "badger warrior."

SWIMMERS VS. NON-SWIMMERS

✦ Although most dogs can swim, some breeds would have extreme difficulty doing so because of their conformation, such as the Basset Hound, with its heavy body and short legs.

✦ Many breeds of dog are good swimmers, but Newfoundlands are amazing swimmers. A newspaper article published shortly after the sinking of the Titanic told the story of a black Newfoundland called Rigel. Belonging to an officer who went down with the ship, the dog swam for hours, and alerted the rescue ship Carpathia to one of the lifeboats by his barking.

The sound of the waves is so relaxing. Time for a nap, I think.

WEBBED PAWS

Many dogs bred to work in water have webbed paws, including:

* Akita
* Brussels Griffon
* Chesapeake Bay Retriever
* Field Spaniel
* German Pointer
* Irish Water Spaniel
* Labrador Retriever
* Leonberger
* Newfoundland
* Norwegian Buhund
* Nova Scotia Duck Tolling Retriever
* Otterhound
* Poodle
* Portuguese Water Dog
* Spanish Water Dog
* Weimaraner
* Wire-haired Pointing Griffon

A tired Basset Hound puppy on the beach.

Famed with fishermen as a life saver, the Newfoundland's webbed feet and oily coat allow it to remain in the water for long periods.

WORLD'S BIGGEST KENNEL? In the 13th century, the Mongol emperor Kublai Khan owned 5,000 Mastiffs for use in hunting and war—the most dogs ever owned by one person.

English Mastiff

WORLD'S BIGGEST DOG

+ Aicama Zorba of La-Susa, an English Mastiff from London, England, set the record as the world's biggest ever dog in 1989. Zorba weighed 343 pounds (156 kg), and measured 37 inches (94 cm) from shoulder to paw and 99 inches (251 cm) from nose to tail tip.

+ Zorba's record as the heaviest dog still stands after his death. Guinness World Records no longer considers claims for heaviest or lightest dogs in case this encourages owners to over- or underfeed their pets.

This 2nd-century A.D. Roman statue of a dog in the British Museum in London is widely considered to be a Molossus.

The Molossus

+ The Molossus is an extinct dog breed, named after an ancient Greek tribe, the Molossi. This fierce dog is believed to have been used by the ancient Greeks and Romans as a war dog, fighting dog, hunter, and guard.

+ The Molossus is generally considered to be a very large Mastiff-type dog. As well as modern Mastiffs, several other breeds are believed to descend from the Molossus, including the Bulldog, Great Dane, Bernese Mountain Dog, Swiss Mountain Dog, and St. Bernard.

BENEFITS OF NEUTER SURGERY

Although all types of surgery have inherent risks, neutering does prevent many potential health problems in later life, in addition to its other benefits.

❶ Many dogs escape from their homes and backyards in order to wander the streets in search of a mate. When this happens, the dog is typically in heat and will do anything possible to get close to another dog. When a dog is experiencing the intensity of being in heat, it may become lost if it wanders too far from home. If you choose to have your dog neutered, it will become calmer and less likely to try to escape.

❷ There is a major problem with overpopulation of domestic animals, mostly cats and dogs. By having your dog neutered, you will be helping to alleviate the problem of unwanted puppies being born.

❸ Studies show that neutering greatly reduces the risk of diseases such as testicular cancer in male dogs, and ovarian or uterine cancer in female dogs. These are just a few of the possible diseases that are more prominent in animals that remain unneutered.

❹ Most house pets are very calm and do not seek fights with other animals. However, when dogs are not neutered, they are more susceptible to engaging in violent interactions with other dogs. Most dog fights happen between animals that have not been neutered. By having your

dog neutered, you are reducing the risk of your pet getting hurt in a fight.

❺ Last but not least, a neutered female dog will not have menstruation periods that require cleaning up. Although it does not happen often and varies from breed to breed, a female dog's menstruation cycle will be eliminated once she is neutered.

Neutering helps to prevent dogs from fighting.

DOGS ON ALBUM COVERS
- Sublime's "What I Got..." EP and "Greatest Hits" compilation
- Alice in Chains's self-titled album
- Bad Religion's "Recipe For Hate"
- Eric Clapton's "There's One In Every Crowd"

A Cocker Spaniel cools down in a puddle of water— and gets thoroughly dirty in the process.

Oooo, that feels good—and humans always smell better after I've given them a shower.

WHY DO DOGS ROLL AROUND IN THE DIRTIEST OF THINGS?

❂ Dogs find feces of all sorts very interesting. This is because the feces conveys information about the animal that deposited it, such as species and sex. Dogs simply do not consider feces dirty and embarrassing as humans do. Rolling in feces appears to be a reaction to the scent, and is normal canine behavior.

❂ Dogs also get smelly from swimming and bathing in dirty water, and digging in the yard. The dog may be cooling itself in the water, curious about what is hidden in the ground, or simply having fun playing.

❂ Smell is a primal sense, and it is hard to account for who likes what. Just as some people enjoy the smell of strong cheeses but others do not, dogs may revel in smells that most humans find objectionable. It is hard to criticize their tastes, because they have millions more scent receptors than we do. Therefore, it is possible that they detect pleasing odors of which humans are completely unaware.

Stay clear of a wet dog or it will thoroughly soak you with whatever it has been swimming in when it shakes itself dry.

Dachshund

Pet Passports

+ The Pet Travel Scheme (PETS) allows dogs to travel between member countries without quarantine, as long as certain conditions are met. These conditions include booking the trip with an approved transport company, using an approved route, and fulfilling certain health-related criteria.

+ You need to prepare at least 7–8 months before you travel. To qualify for the scheme, your pet must comply with several conditions, including having a microchip implant. The dog must also be vaccinated against rabies, and have the correct vaccination certification. A blood test may be required to show that the vaccine has given the dog satisfactory protection. In addition, the dog must have an official PETS certificate issued by a government-authorized veterinarian.

TRAVEL CRATES
Make sure that you use a suitable travel crate for your dog, with adequate ventilation and approved containers for food and water. There are no standardized rules, so check requirements carefully each time you travel.

DOGS IN SPACE

* In the early days of spaceflight, animals were sent into space to test the feasibility of sending humans. In the 1950s and 1960s, the Soviets used female stray dogs as their preferred animal.

* The first dogs to make a suborbital flight were Dezik and Tsygan in 1951. Both dogs returned unharmed, although Dezik died during another flight later that year.

* Perhaps the most famous Soviet space dog is Laika, who was the first living creature to complete an orbital spaceflight aboard Sputnik 2 in 1957. For nearly 50 years, the official report was that she died after oxygen supplies ran out, but in 2002 it was revealed that Laika died 5–7 hours into the flight due to overheating.

Commemorative Mongolian stamps featuring Soviet space dog Laika.

Tips for a Well-behaved Dog

- Start training a puppy as early as the seventh week. Older dogs have acquired bad habits that may be hard to break.

- Instill toilet training rules as early as possible.

- Train the dog as humanely as possible, and use positive, motivational methods. Include "play training," using constructive games to make it more fun and enjoyable for both you and the dog.

- Let the dog know that rules and commands are not optional. Do not impose rules or give commands that you cannot enforce. Consistency matters when dealing with discipline.

- Train the dog to follow any command the first time it is given. Repeating commands demonstrates to the dog that the first command is a bluff, and the dog can ignore it.

- Give clear and specific commands. Combined commands that have incompatible meanings will confuse the dog. For example, "Sit" and "Down" are two different commands and should not be combined to "Sit down."

- Use a calm, authoritative voice when giving commands to the dog. You should not have to shout to be heard or obeyed. The dog must be able to recognize the authority in your command without your being harsh or loud.

- Use the dog's name positively, so that when its name is called, the dog knows that good things are about to happen. The sound of its name should inspire enthusiasm, not fear.

Be patient when training puppies. Their natural curiosity can lead to mishaps.

- Correct misbehavior without punishment. Communicating and teaching the dog good behavior through motivation is more fun and effective. Dominating the dog with harsh punishment will weaken your relationship.

- Precise timing is important when training a dog. After-the-fact discipline does not work. Discipline should be given at the time the misbehavior is committed.

Dogs respond well to calm, clear, and consistent training techniques. You will get a much better response, and greater enjoyment for both you and your pet, if you use positive encouragement to instill good behavior.

- Never train a dog when you are angry, grouchy, or impatient. You cannot earn a dog's respect by yelling, hitting, or being cruel. Never instigate fear in the dog with your demeanor.

- Language is not important to dogs. While they may learn the meaning of some words, they understand nonverbal signs like voice quality, gestures, and body stance better than words.

- When a dog obeys a command, give it a big smile and praise it with a cheery voice. Let the dog know how pleased you are. If the dog did not obey, give it a dirty look and say a stern "No" in a low voice.

- For the most effective results when training and communicating with a dog, your facial expression, eyes, and tone of voice must say the same thing. Remember that a dog can read your body language accurately.

WALKING TO HEEL

☆ *A dog that walks to heel—that is, alongside its owner rather than pulling at the leash—is a pleasure to take out. You can start teaching a dog to walk to heel in the yard without a leash. Walk around, holding a treat in your hand so that the dog knows it is there. This will cause the dog to walk beside you, and as it does, say "Heel" several times and give it treats.*

☆ *Once this is established, keep the treats out of sight, but still reward the dog for walking to heel. Next, practice the exercise with the dog on a leash. Walking to heel is a boring exercise for the dog, so keep the training sessions to about five minutes.*

☆ *There are two main reasons why dogs pull away when on a leash. One is to reach a goal quickly, such as its favorite location. The other is that the dog considers itself to be in charge of the walk. To correct the behavior, as your dog starts to pull on the leash, begin to walk backward. This will tighten the leash and surprise the dog, who will come trotting back. When it does, reward and praise the dog.*

Body language is more important than the words you use when training a dog.

Regal Canines

+ According to Pliny the Elder in his *Naturalis Historiae* (Natural History), published around 77 A.D., an African people called the Ptoemphani had a dog as their king, and interpreted his commands from his movements.

+ The Chinese Shang Dynasty queen Fu Hao was buried in a lacquered coffin above a pit containing the remains of six dogs. The tomb dates from around 1250 B.C.

+ The 430 B.C. tomb of Yi, the Chinese marquis of the state of Zeng in the modern-day Hubei Province, had a dog in its own coffin.

+ Dowager Empress Tzu Hsi (1835–1908) of the Manchu Dynasty of China supervised the breeding of the palace dogs—including Pekingese, Shih Tzu, and Pugs—and even wrote about them in poems.

+ The French queen Marie Antoinette was very fond of Papillons, and also had a Pug called Mops. She reputedly went to the guillotine in 1793 carrying her favorite dog.

+ The French empress Josephine had a favorite Pug called Fortuné that is alleged to have bitten her husband, Napoleon Bonaparte, on their wedding night. During an imprisonment in 1794 before her marriage, the dog was the only visitor that Josephine was allowed to have, and it is reputed that she hid messages to her family under the dog's collar.

+ When Anne Boleyn, second queen of the infamous English monarch Henry VIII, was executed in 1536, she asked that her favorite dog, a Greyhound named Urian, be with her to provide comfort.

+ Mary Queen of Scots was locked up in the Tower of London with her dogs when she became a prisoner of Elizabeth I of England. When she was executed in 1587, one of her dogs accompanied her, concealed in her long skirt. The dog reputedly refused to leave Mary's body after the execution.

+ The British queen Victoria asked for her favorite Pomeranian, Turi, on her deathbed in 1901. The favorite dog of Victoria's successor, Edward VII, was a Wire Fox Terrier named Caesar, who even took part in the king's funeral procession.

+ The British queen Elizabeth II is famously associated with Corgis. She was given her own Pembroke Welsh Corgi, called Susan, for her 18th birthday in 1944, and has owned more than 30 Corgis since that date, many the descendants of Susan.

The Pug was a favorite of French royalty, with both Marie Antoinette and Josephine Bonaparte owning Pugs.

Reward Training

+ Dogs learn much more quickly (and
less traumatically) if they are rewarded
for getting something right rather than
punished for getting something wrong.
Training based on a reward system for
the correct responses enables dogs to
learn in a positive way what humans
want to teach them.

+ A dog's behavior is determined by the
result that the behavior brings, so if a
certain behavior is followed by a good
experience, that behavior will tend to
be repeated. Conversely, if behavior is
ignored and nothing gained from it,
it will die out.

+ Most dogs are very food-oriented,
and small tasty treats make excellent
rewards when training. These can be
part of the dog's daily food ration or
be healthy additions, such as pieces
of carrot or morsels of baked liver.

+ Lavish praise is also essential. All dogs
want approval from the pack leader—
verbal praise and possibly physical
contact are great encouragement.

Operant
conditioning

Classical
conditioning

LEARNING THEORY

Dogs respond to both classical and
operant conditioning techniques.

• "Classical conditioning" relates to
involuntary responses, such as
salivating when dinner is served.

• "Operant conditioning" relates to
voluntary responses, such as a dog
sitting for a treat.

A Dalmatian
struggles to resist
temptation. Dogs
are very food-
oriented. When
given to a dog in
the correct way,
tasty treats can
be used to train
the dog to follow
commands and
display good
behavior.

CLICKER TRAINING

Clicker

❋ Clicker training is the most recent method in the dog training evolution. Heavily connected to operant conditioning, it is a humane and effective method of shaping dog behavior.

❋ Clicker training is a positive reward technique that depends on cooperation, consistency, and repetition. The dog learns to respond to positive consequences and avoid negative ones.

❋ The clicker is a toy-like device with a metal strip that provides a quick, clear, and distinctive clicking sound when pressed. The clicker is pressed while a desired behavior is happening, rather than afterward, and the click is accompanied by a reward, such as a food treat. The dog comes to associate the sound of the clicker with a desired behavior and a reward for that behavior.

❋ The learning theory combines both negative reinforcement (punishment) and positive reinforcement (reward). As dogs learn to maintain behavior that is rewarded, they also learn to inhibit behavior that is punished.

A Rhodesian Ridgeback responds beautifully to clicker training.

LURE TRAINING

★ This training method uses an object that appeals to the dog (toys, treats, and so on) to train the dog to follow obedience commands (such as "Sit," "Down," or "Heel"). The lure is gradually phased out as the learning progresses.

★ In lure training, the trainer gives a command and then moves the lure in order to direct the dog to follow the command. For example, the trainer says "Sit" and then moves the lure above the dog's head. As the dog raises its head to watch the lure, the dog naturally lowers its rear end and sits down. The trainer then rewards the dog.

★ This is an outstanding motivational approach and is frequently successful where other training methods have failed, especially for puppies, sensitive dogs, timid dogs, and aggressive or difficult-to-train dogs.

A lure can be a dog's favorite chew toy or food reward.

Growling

+ A dog's growl can mean several things. It is usually a warning, meaning "Leave me alone," and often indicates anxiety about a situation.

+ A growl may be disciplinary—pack leaders keep younger dogs under control by looks and growls before they ever need to nip them.

+ The usual reason a dog on a leash growls at another dog is fear. A dog off the leash has the potential to escape or fight, but a dog on a leash does not have these options and may adopt a policy of aggression in order to scare the other dog away.

+ A dog growling during play may simply be playful. It is important to differentiate this sort of growl from a more dominant one. If a dog wins a game with its owner that involved growling, it can extend to other situations; for example, the dog that growls when the owner attempts to move it off the couch. If the owner becomes frightened by the growling, the dog will learn to growl to get its own way.

Growls can mean several things, so pay attention to the situation to learn what your dog is saying.

A dog on a leash may growl because it is frightened, but cannot flee or fight.

FEAR AGGRESSION

Aggression in dogs is usually the result of fear, and the aggressive dog is simply trying to make the object of its fear go away. Fear aggression can take a lot of time and patience to overcome. Here are some tips.

❶ Never shout at or hit the dog when it is showing fear aggression. This would only make the problem worse.

❷ Do not reassure the dog, because this could appear to be praising it for the aggressive behavior.

❸ Remain calm and relaxed. This will convey itself to the dog, whereas anxiety on your part will only worsen the situation.

❹ The dog needs gentle and repeated exposure to the thing that it fears, combined with a good experience, such as receiving a treat from visitors or much praise when it does not bark at another dog.

DOMINANCE AGGRESSION

✶ Dogs are pack animals. The pack gives them support and protection. The pack of the pet dog is the family of people and other animals with which it lives.

✶ For a dog to be happy and acceptable to the rest of the pack, it needs a set of rules to live by. In the wild, these would be maintained by the stronger members of the pack. In the domestic situation, the humans take these roles.

✶ For humans and dogs to live together successfully, the dog must be inferior to all human family members of the pack. Failure to impose this hierarchy can cause the dog to consider itself dominant to its owners. As a result, the dog will be difficult to train, behave in ways that are not socially acceptable in the family situation, and may even be dangerous.

DOMINANCE TRAINING (FOR OWNERS)

Not all dogs are the dominant type, but for those that are, prevention is easier than cure, and early establishment of a dog's place in the family pack will mean a happier relationship in the long term.

❶ Walk through doorways in front of your dog. Do not step over or walk around the dog if it is in the way. Make the dog move.

❷ Do not let the dog into your bedroom or onto your bed. Occasionally go and sit in the dog's bed. Do not allow the dog onto laps or furniture.

❸ Never feed the dog from your plate or while you are eating. Feed the dog its own food after you have eaten.

❹ Always win any games. Give the dog attention when you initiate it, not when the dog asks for it.

This Dogue de Bordeaux puppy knows its place in the pack—it sleeps in a dog bed, not on its owner's.

Visiting the Veterinarian

You should get your dog checked by a veterinarian at least twice a year. If you have an elderly dog, it might need more frequent checkups. If the dog displays any symptoms that you are unsure about, always consult a veterinarian—it never hurts to telephone the veterinarian's surgery for advice.

SYMPTOMS TO LOOK OUT FOR

Watching out for symptoms of illness is an important part of your pet's health care. Consult a veterinarian if you notice any of the following:

- Eating less food than usual
- Vomiting
- Limping
- Coughing
- Scratching more frequently than usual
- Severe diarrhea or constipation

WHAT TO TREAT FROM HOME

✦ If your dog has a small wound or abrasion, trim the hair from the area, wash the wound, and apply a strong antibiotic.

✦ You can treat diarrhea in an adult dog, as long as the dog is not behaving differently and there is no blood in the stool. Fast the dog for 24 hours, but make sure that fresh water is available at all times. Then give the dog a bland diet, such as plain cooked fish or chicken and rice, in three to four small meals a day, until the feces are normal. Gradually return the dog to its regular diet over the course of the next few days, keeping an eye out for any changes.

SYMPTOMS OF POISONING

Poisons abound in every home. Potentially lethal substances include detergents and disinfectants. The typical responses to ingestion of poison are dilated pupils, difficulty breathing, muscle tremors, and a swollen abdomen. In a case of suspected poisoning, seek veterinary help as soon as possible.

A veterinarian giving a young Labrador Retriever a checkup.

COMMON DOG INJURIES

✦ **Paw injuries**—Pus indicates that the wound is infected, and must be treated by a veterinarian.

✦ **Tail injuries**—If infected, these need to be treated professionally.

✦ **Spinal injuries**—Do not move the dog until you are certain of the extent of the injuries.

Medicine Warning
Never give a dog human medicine. This can cause very serious side effects and even death. Always consult a veterinarian prior to giving a dog any animal medication.

HOW TO BANDAGE A DOG

❶ Clean and disinfect the wound, place a pad of cotton on it, and then wrap the wound with a gauze bandage.

❷ Making sure that the bandage is not too loose or tight, apply a layer of adhesive bandage over the gauze. To try to prevent the bandage from slipping, you can add a few strips of household sticky tape across the bandage and nearby fur.

❸ Check the bandage regularly and change it on schedule. Make sure that the bandage remains clean, and cover it with something waterproof when the dog goes outside.

FIRST-AID KIT

It is always best to be prepared by having a canine first-aid kit around. Here are some things to include.

☆ Suitable container

☆ Sterile saline solution

☆ Nonstick, absorbent cotton pads

☆ Gauze and adhesive bandages

☆ Tweezers

☆ Splint

☆ Clean water and bowl

☆ Muzzle

☆ Thermometer

☆ Latex gloves

☆ Blanket

☆ Emergency telephone numbers

A Pug with a bandaged paw.

Dogs in Comics

+ A St. Bernard named Andy is the trusty companion of Mark Trail, a journalist whose assignments for an outdoor magazine lead to dangerous adventures in the *Mark Trail* comic strip, introduced in 1946.

+ *Beetle Bailey*, launched in 1950, relates the comic mishaps of a lazy soldier called Beetle Bailey. His supervisor and nemesis, Sergeant Snorkel, has a human-like dog called Otto.

+ Snoopy, who first appeared in the *Peanuts* cartoon strip in 1950, is the pet Beagle of the main character Charlie Brown. Snoopy communicates through "thought bubbles," and lives an exciting fantasy life in his daydreams, from being a World War I Flying Ace to Joe Cool. Snoopy is now one of the most popular and well-known cartoon characters.

+ Dogmatix made his first appearance in the French *Asterix* comic book series in 1963. Dogmatix is the tiny white pet dog of the obese and superhumanly strong Obelix. The title character Asterix often disagrees with Obelix over whether Dogmatix should accompany them on their adventures.

+ The *Garfield* comic strip, which debuted in 1978, is about a cynical cat called Garfield. One of Garfield's favorite pastimes is to torment Odie, a naive yellow Beagle who drools a lot.

A Snoopy balloon in the guise of one of his alter egos, a World War I Flying Ace, at Macy's Thanksgiving Day Parade in New York.

POCKET BEAGLES

In the 16th century, Queen Elizabeth I of England kept numous Beagles, some of which were so small that they could be put in one's pocket and so became known as Pocket Beagles. True Pocket Beagles are now extinct.

A still from the 2006 animated movie "Asterix and the Vikings," featuring the tiny but fearless Dogmatix.

Chinese Fu dog statues are symbols of protection, and are usually placed at an entrance.

FU DOGS

Also called Chinese lion dogs, Fu lions, or guardian lions, these are pairs of statues that are traditionally found flanking the entrance to palaces, temples, and other buildings. Since lions are not indigenous to China, it is believed that ancient Chinese sculptors modeled these lion statues on Chinese dog breeds, such as the Chow Chow. The male statue is always on the right side of the entrance and rests his right paw on a ball; the female statue is always on the left side of the entrance and rests her left paw on a cub. Fu dogs are also found in pottery and other decorative arts.

CRAZY CANINE LAWS

Anchorage, Alaska

No one may tie their pet dog to the roof of a car.

California

In some areas of California, animals are banned from mating publicly within 1,500 feet (457 m) of a tavern, school, or place of worship.

Belvedere, California

"No dog shall be in a public place without its master on a leash."

Ventura County, California

Cats and dogs are not allowed to mate without a permit.

Denver, Colorado

The dog catcher must notify dogs of impounding by posting, for three consecutive days, a notice on a tree in the city park and along a public road running through said park.

Hartford, Connecticut

It is illegal to educate dogs.

Continued on page 149

It would be illegal to educate this Dachshund puppy in Hartford, Connecticut.

 BREED GROUPS

✤ The first dogs were bred selectively for a specific purpose, such as herding livestock or dispeling vermin. By the middle of the 19th century, with interest in dogs steadily increasing, the need for a system of grouping breeds into categories became apparent. The current system has generally been developed to take into account the type of work, if any, and the size of breeds.

✤ Breed group categories and the breeds included within them are defined by kennel clubs. Breed groups vary from organization to organization. For example, the American Kennel Club organizes breeds into seven breed groups, while the Fédération Cynologique Internationale organizes them into ten groups.

✤ Breed groups are of great help in categorizing breeds for exhibition purposes, and also in aiding the purchaser to select the breed best suited to the purpose that he or she has in mind, be it a children's pet, hunting dog, or guard.

BIKEJORING AND CANICROSS

☆ *Bikejoring is a competitive or recreational sport in which a harnessed dog or team of dogs tows a cyclist. Both cyclist and dog (or dogs) provide power.*

☆ *Canicross is similar to bikejoring, but the dog (or dogs) tow a cross-country runner instead of a cyclist.*

A pet owner takes his dog biking, using a special leash attachment so that he can keep both hands safely on the handlebars.

Biking with Your Dog

+ Regardless of the size or breed of your dog, most dogs love to run. If you enjoy riding a bicycle, then why not take your dog with you (if it can keep up to speed)? It is a wonderful way of spending time with your pet, while getting some exercise yourself.

+ The safest and easiest way to ride a bike with a dog is to make sure that you keep your pet on a leash. There are many special bike leash products available that can be attached under the bike seat. This allows you to keep both hands on the handlebars, offering comfort and protection for both you and the dog.

+ The dog is less likely to get bothered by distractions if it has good obedience. Make sure that the dog knows commands like "Off" and "Leave" before you begin the ride. Also, make sure that you bring along the dog's favorite treats or toy. Whenever the dog comes across a distraction, tell it to "Leave" and then give the dog a snack or offer a distraction.

+ If you like to ride along special bike trails and tracks, bringing along your dog is one of the best treats your pet could imagine.

With a little basic training, the dog can be a great companion for a mountain biker. In fact, there are lots of mountain biking routes where dogs can run free without a leash, as long as the owner keeps the dog under control.

WET NOSE
A dog's wet nose aids heat loss through evaporation.

A sheepdog panting to cool down. As air passes over the moist surfaces of the nose and mouth, it takes up moisture and, with it, heat. By panting rapidly and hanging out the tongue, the rate of heat loss is increased.

REGULATING BODY TEMPERATURE

☆ Dogs do not regulate their body temperature in the same way as humans. While humans sweat or have goosebumps to regulate interior temperature, dogs do so by panting. This occurs as the heat is transferred from the hottest place in the body. It is actually much more effective than the human sweating mechanism.

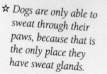

☆ Dogs are only able to sweat through their paws, because that is the only place they have sweat glands.

BIO-DETECTION DOGS

✴ Dogs have an amazing sense of smell, and with the correct training, may be useful in diagnosing diseases. Such dogs are known as bio-detection dogs, and are used for such things as detecting the odors given off by a diabetic person whose blood sugar level is dropping dangerously low.

✴ The use of bio-detection dogs to detect cancer is also being studied. Some studies have shown up to a 99 percent accuracy rate for bio-detection dogs trained to detect lung cancer, and similarly high results for breast cancer, even in its earliest stages. However, other cancers have proved difficult to detect.

✴ Currently, many of these techniques are experimental and are still being investigated, with the intention of discovering what substances the disease processes give off that the dogs detect. The hope is that tests can then be developed for use in the laboratory, perhaps similar to the way that the breathalyzer detects alcohol.

Continued from page 146

Crazy Canine Laws

Illinois

It is illegal to give a dog whiskey.

Chicago, Illinois

It is illegal to take a French Poodle to the opera.

Northbrook, Illinois

It is illegal for dogs to bark for more than 15 minutes.

Zion, Illinois

It is illegal for anyone to give lighted cigars to dogs, cats, or other domesticated animals kept as pets.

Fort Thomas, Kentucky

Dogs may not molest cars.

Michigan

It is illegal to kill a dog using a decompression chamber.

Palding, Ohio

A police officer may bite a dog to quiet it.

Continued on page 150

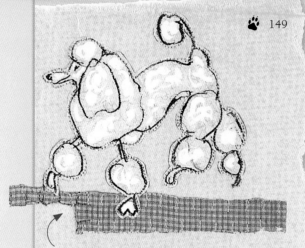

No matter how fancy its hairstyle, a Poodle is not allowed to go to the opera in Illinois.

Cigar-smoking dog: illegal in Illinois.

The Saluki is esteemed in Muslim cultures for its speed and beauty.

CLEANEST BREED

Dogs are considered unclean in many Muslim cultures. If licked by a dog, a Muslim is required to wash the area seven times before praying. The only exception is the Saluki, an ancient sight hound related to the Greyhound, which is highly valued as a fleet-footed hunter and considered cleaner than other breeds.

CATS AND DOGS

A new dog must be taught to respect a cat and to leave it alone—for the safety of both animals. To allow the dog to become familiar with the cat safely, place the cat in a crate that is raised off the floor, or put the dog in a house cage. The dog should be rewarded for not pestering the cat. Within a few days, dogs and cats usually settle down together, and many even become firm friends.

If introduced to each other carefully, cats and dogs can become great friends.

Continued from page 149

Crazy Canine Laws

Oklahoma

In some areas of Oklahoma, people who make ugly faces at dogs may be fined and/or jailed.

Oklahoma

Dogs must have a permit signed by the mayor in order to congregate in groups of three or more on private property.

North Carolina

Laws applying to some areas of North Carolina prohibit fights between cats and dogs.

Cerberus

In Greek mythology, the gates of the underworld are guarded by the god Hades and his three-headed hound of hell, Cerberus.

Hades

Cerberus

A German short-haired Pointer competing in a field trial.

Field Trials

✦ A field trial is a competitive event in which hunting dogs compete against one another. Field trials are usually organized by kennel clubs or other hunting dog organizations.

✦ The term "hunting dog" refers to any dog that assists humans in hunting. There are several types of hunting dogs developed for various tasks. They include hounds, gundogs, and terriers.

FOX HUNTING

The sport of fox hunting originated in Britain in the 1500s, and eventually reached most countries worldwide. Fox hunting involves the locating, chasing, and killing of a red fox by a group of riders and their trained fox hounds. In 2004, fox hunting was banned in England and Wales through the activist efforts of those who felt that the sport was cruel and unnecessary. In the United States, the sport is now called fox chasing. The fox is chased (for the thrill of the chase), but not killed.

FRIENDSHIP OMEN
According to folklore, if a strange dog walks into your home, it indicates that you will soon meet someone new who will become a great friend.

Vintage photograph of a pack of fox hounds.

THE LANDSEER

The particolored variety of the Newfoundland dog is known as the Landseer, named after the Victorian painter Sir Edwin Landseer. The artist depicted them in several paintings in celebration of their skills as water rescue dogs.

Stamp featuring a French Renaissance painting of the Roman goddess Diana with a hunting hound.

Gs. 0.25

CORREO DEL PARAGUAY

"A Distinguished Member of the Humane Society" (1838) by Sir Edwin Landseer is a portrait of a Newfoundland that was famous for many water rescues.

Dogs in Art

Dogs have been depicted in art since prehistoric times, and continue to be very popular subjects for artists today.

+ Dogs were domesticated in many parts of the prehistoric world, and were depicted in cave paintings. Paintings of hunters and dogs in the Lascaux caves of France date back 17,000 years. Cave paintings in Spain depicting dogs and doglike creatures date back over 12,000 years.

+ There is pictorial evidence dating to 6000 B.C. of a Mesopotamian Greyhound type that could run down prey.

+ Egyptian wall paintings that are 6,600 years old feature domesticated dogs that resemble Greyhounds and Bullmastiffs.

+ In ancient Greek and Roman art, there are numerous images on pottery and in sculpture of dogs wearing collars and working as hunters and guards.

+ The medieval Bayeux Tapestry, a 76-yard (70-m) long embroidered cloth depicting the Norman conquest of England in 1066, features 55 dogs.

+ Dogs were often featured in Renaissance paintings and tapestries, usually as part of allegorical, religious, or mythological subjects. A variety of breeds were depicted, including retrievers, spaniels and Greyhounds.

Pueblo cave painting showing a doglike creature.

+ From the Renaissance onward, kings and queens were frequently painted with their loyal four-legged companions at their feet. By the Victorian era, children and dogs were another popular subject for artists.

+ In the 1800s, dog portraiture became popular, and canines featured prominently in the works of Thomas Gainsborough, Sir Edwin Landseer, and George Stubbs, as well as in the art of American folk painters such as Amni Phillips and William Henry Brown.

Bronze statue of dogs hunting wild boar in a courtyard in the ancient Roman city of Pompeii in Italy.

Myths About Dog Behavior

❶ When dogs are angry with people, they do all kinds of horrible things.
Remember that a dog is a dog, and it is natural for it to dig, to bark, to run around, to chase other dogs, and so on. The dog is not doing these things because it is angry or wants to get back at you. It is best if you try to understand the cause of the dog's behavior. As a social animal, most undesirable behavior stems from the frustration of being left alone.

Dogs look guilty in response to human body language, not because they know they have done something wrong.

❷ Dogs hate to be crated.
Dogs are den animals by nature, and when properly trained, most dogs love to be crated. The crate is their peaceful sanctuary and it is useful when the family is away.

❸ Dogs look guilty after they have done something wrong.
Dogs react to human body language and emotions. Dogs can read human emotions and body language accurately, and know when we are upset or angry. They try to appease our feelings by crawling on the floor, crouching, rolling over on their backs, or avoiding eye contact.

❹ Punish the dog for growling or it will become aggressive.
Growling is a dog's way of communicating to us that something is disturbing them. Punishing them will not get rid of the disturbing feeling, but will stop them from growling as a warning, which may end in disaster. It would be better to help the dog overcome its feelings for something or someone that disturbs it.

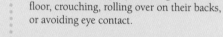

Dogs regard a crate as their den, and feel safe inside it.

Chew toy

❺ If you give chew toys to a dog, it will learn to chew everything.

Dogs learn how to distinguish their toys from forbidden items with minimal training. Chewing is an outlet for a lonely and bored dog. Chew toys give the dog something to do, thereby preventing misbehavior.

❻ You have to show the dog who is boss.

This is true to the extent that in the dog's perception, you must be the pack leader. However, you do not have show it through dominant behaviors such as yelling, striking, or other harsh methods of punishment. Be the dog's leader by showing it what to do and how to behave. Generally, dogs assume the "top dog" position if their owners fail to do so.

❼ In a multi-dog household, give more attention to the dominant dogs to support the hierarchy.

No valuable positive behavioral effects are achieved by this attitude. Aggressive dogs must be taught to develop a happy emotional response to other dogs by conditioning.

❽ Dogs that are abused as a puppy are aggressive/fearful/shy.

Fearful or shy behaviors in dogs are inherited traits, although the manifestation of these traits can be influenced by learning and the environment. Dogs can be trained to cast off their fears, but the training should be started as soon as the problem is identified to avoid more damage.

A shy puppy with its favorite chew toy.

Please come home soon. I'm lonely.

Toilet Training

Puppies need to be toilet trained, and this will usually take a lot of patience on your part. If you are buying a puppy that is more than 7 weeks old, choose one that has started toilet training with its breeder. Grown-up dogs can be toilet trained in the same way as puppies.

+ Puppies have inadequate bladder control. Take the puppy outside frequently for the first few months, until the puppy learns that going to the toilet is an activity for outside and not in the middle of your floor.

+ Dogs perform better when they have a routine schedule. Feed the puppy on schedule, and always take it to the designated relief spot after feeding. Do not play with the puppy until after it relieves itself.

+ Puppies usually have to go to the toilet when they wake up in the morning or after a snooze, within half an hour of eating, and before they go to sleep.

+ Use a crate or a baby gate to confine the puppy when you cannot watch it. Restrict the puppy in a room with tile or other washable flooring, not in a room with a carpeted floor.

+ Dogs and puppies prefer to be clean and to sleep in a tidy area. Puppies and dogs that soil the house indiscriminately do so because they were not taught to do otherwise. Toilet training failures are the fault of humans, not the dog.

The basis of successful toilet training is to provide the puppy with frequent opportunities to relieve itself in an appropriate place.

FALSE PREGNANCY

Sometimes a non-pregnant female will go through a period of pseudo-pregnancy, known as false pregnancy. During this time, she may gain weight, have mammary gland development, produce milk, and exhibit nesting behaviors.

False pregnancy is a normal physiological state for a female dog. A veterinarian may treat severe cases with drugs.

The bronze statue of Balto, by sculptor Frederick Roth, in Central Park in New York.

The name Basenji means "bush thing," and the breed originates from central Africa.

 ## BALTO

★ Balto was a Siberian Husky that led a sled dog team across Alaska to deliver diphtheria vaccine to the icebound port of Nome in 1925. The annual Iditarod Trail Sled Dog Race commemorates the journey.

★ Erected in 1925, a statue of Balto can be found in New York's Central Park in honor of the dog's heroic actions.

★ The animated film *Balto* was released 1995. In the movie, Balto is half-dog, half-wolf—and shunned by all. Balto goes on to become a hero when he travels many miles to deliver diphtheria serum to a hospital full of sick children.

Yodelayheehoo!

The Basenji is famed for the fact that it does not bark, although some Basenjis do make a yodeling sound when excited. The dog is also famous for washing itself like a cat.

Endoparasites

Endoparasites—that is, organisms that live inside another living organism—can seriously affect the health of a dog, or even kill it. There are many excellent antiparasitic drugs, or "dewormers," available, but it is advisable to discuss their use with a veterinarian.

✦ **Roundworms—**
Roundworms spend their time floating inside the dog's liver, heart, and lungs. When they mature, they make their home inside the small intestines, where they continually feed on the food that the dog eats. Signs that a dog may be infested with roundworms include gas, enormous surges in appetite, diarrhea, and bloating.

✦ **Whipworms—**These can be found living inside the dog's large intestine, which is where the worms also reproduce. Dogs can become infected with whipworms by eating the infected stools of other dogs. Sometimes, a dog can become infested with whipworms after stepping in infected dog feces and then licking its paws. Whipworms can cause the dog to have diarrhea, bloody stools, dry fur, and increased appetite.

✦ **Tapeworms—**Like other internal parasites, tapeworms can cause the dog to have increased appetite levels, weight loss, rectal inflammation/itching, and visible signs of the worms from the orifices of the dog's body. Tapeworms look like little pieces of white rice that can easily be seen on the dog's stools, and even sometimes coming out of areas like the ears.

✦ **Hookworms—**A dog can pick up this parasite from eating the stools of other animals that have been infected. Hookworms can cause symptoms such as gas, loose stools, increased appetite, and dry, brittle fur. These parasites spend most of their time feeding off the food the dog eats, as well as sucking the blood from the dog.

✦ **Giardia—**These internal parasites are typically picked up from areas of water, such as a small pond or lake. The dog can accidentally pick up this creature from swimming, and once ingested, the parasites live and eat at the inner lining of the dog's small intestine. This causes inflammation, mucus-covered stools, weight loss, and bloating.

Hookworm

Tapeworm

Giardia

A bronze plaque of a dog on the Charles Bridge in Prague.

FAITHFUL SPOUSE

The Charles Bridge in Prague in the Czech Republic, which began construction in 1357, is decorated with numerous statues and plaques. One plaque shows a guard rubbing a dog's head. It has become popular for visitors to rub the dog to ensure that a spouse will remain faithful.

GREYHOUND RACING

❀ With its keen eyesight and great speed, the Greyhound has been highly valued as a sight hound for coursing (hunting prey by catching it at speed) since ancient Egyptian times, when it was depicted on the tombs of pharaohs.

❀ The Greyhound is now also a competitor on the race track. It is able to run so fast because of its light, muscular build, large heart, extremely flexible spine, and high percentage of fast-twitch muscles.

❀ Looking like a Greyhound in miniature, the Whippet is another extremely fast dog, and was bred expressly for racing.

Greyhounds chase a mechanical lure around the track. The lure may be a windsock or toy.

If your dog is ruining your backyard by digging holes, provide a sandpit with buried rewards as an alternative.

Housetraining Problems

✦ If your dog changes its customary habits, look for possible causes. It could be a medical problem, a new animal in the household, or a sudden change of environment.

✦ Urinating in different places around the house may be due to a medical problem. Dribbling urine is common among older spayed females; consult a veterinarian.

✦ Chewing is a puppy's way of exploring its environment by tasting whatever it finds. It is also a way to relieve the pain of teething. Provide chewable toys and keep harmful or not-to-be-chewed objects out of reach.

✦ Barking is a dog's way of communicating something. Investigate the causes, and find ways to eliminate unnecessary barking.

✦ Digging may be a way to relieve boredom or to make a cooling/heating pit. Provide a sandbox with buried rewards for this purpose and to discourage digging in other places. Refill the holes the dog previously dug with harmless junk or water.

✦ Training a dog to keep away from the trash bin should start from puppyhood. Keep a tight lid on the trash bin. If the dog is persistent, spray the trash with bitter apple or scatter some jalapeno peppers or something the dog hates onto the trash to keep your pet away.

✦ Make sure that all family members do not feed the dog with scraps from the table, otherwise it will turn into a pest in the dining room and kitchen.

WHAT ARE DOGS SAYING WHEN THEY BARK?

✤ *A bark may be a greeting to a special human.*

✤ *It may be a request to play, or an attention-seeking device.*

✤ *Dogs bark to threaten other animals and people.*

✤ *They may bark to call for company if left alone.*

Barking for attention is often very successful. The natural reaction is to tell the dog to be quiet, or distract it with toys or even food.

Treat = occupied mouth = no
barking—but timing is crucial.

HOW TO STOP A PUPPY FROM CHEWING YOUR SHOES

You can solve this problem by redirecting the chewing toward the dog's toys—instead of your favorite shoes.

✿ Make sure that the dog has plenty of toys to play with and chew on. Get the dog used to chewing on these toys by having them around at all times while the dog is still young. Place them in a confined area with the dog, so that the dog is not tempted to chew other things.

✿ If you see the dog chewing on something it is not supposed to, say "No" and quickly replace the item with a chew toy. Shower the dog with praise when it starts to chew on the toy.

✿ If the dog tries to run off with an item it should not have, such as your shoe, it is simply trying to get some attention. If you ignore the behavior, it will be unproductive and stop.

HOW TO STOP PERSISTENT BARKING

★ *When the dog is barking, ignore it. Do not stroke or talk to the dog, because this will be misconstrued as praise. Do not shout at the dog—it will think you are joining in and will bark even more.*

★ *To teach the dog to be quiet, you must first teach it to bark on command. This can be done by stimulating it to bark, using whatever it would normally bark for, such as its food or a ball. As soon as the dog starts to bark, give a command word, such as "Bark," and reward it. Keep the dog barking for several seconds, if possible. When it takes the reward, it has to stop barking, because its mouth will be otherwise occupied.*

★ *Having established barking to order, you can teach the "Quiet" command. When the dog has been barking for several seconds, pretend you are about to reward it. As it goes quiet to take its reward, say the word "Quiet" and reward it. Practice makes perfect, but the timing in this training exercise is crucial.*

Most puppies go through
a chewing stage
when teething.

WHELPING

Whelping is the process of giving birth to puppies, or whelps. A whelp is a newborn puppy that lacks the ability to see, hear, or regulate its body temperature. Whelps need to be nursed by their mother until they start weaning (the process of moving onto an adult diet from the mother's milk).

A newborn puppy, fast asleep after an exhausting day.

The Whelping Box

❈ The whelping box is the largest and most obvious piece of equipment that you need for a pregnant dog. Dimensions vary, depending on breed and matron size. Manufactured whelping boxes constructed of sturdy plastic may be purchased, although it is easy to make a homemade whelping box with a few basic carpentry skills.

❈ The whelping box must be sturdy, allowing the dam to go in and out with ease. It should be square, because four equal sides allow the dam to position herself comfortably anywhere in the box, while keeping the litter in front of her. The box should allow her to lie fully extended, from the crown of her head to just past her rump, with her legs comfortably extended.

❈ Bigger is not better when it comes to the size of the box, which should not be so enormous that the newborn whelps become disoriented, or "lost" from their mother.

❈ The whelping box should be ready for occupancy about two weeks prior to the litter's due date. Acclimate the matron to the whelping box as her personal territory prior to whelping. Make her bed in the box with old, clean towels, a blanket or sheet, and newspapers that she may shred. Let her become accustomed to getting in and out. If necessary, feed her in the box if she refuses to sleep or rest there.

Place the whelping box in a dark, quiet, draft-free area.

GOOD BREEDS IF…

YOU LOVE GROOMING

- ✿ Chow Chow
- ✿ Japanese Akita
- ✿ Pomeranian
- ✿ Poodle
- ✿ Rough Collie

YOU HATE GROOMING

- ✤ Chinese Crested Dog
- ✤ Smooth-haired Dachshund
- ✤ English Toy Terrier
- ✤ Mexican Hairless Dog (obviously)
- ✤ Pug

NATIONAL TREASURE

The Xoloitzcuintli, or to make it easier the Mexican Hairless Dog or Xolo, is native to South and Central America and Mexico. Once sacred dog to the Aztecs, it is now the national dog of Mexico.

The Mexican Hairless Dog may need to wear a sweater in cold weather.

Poodles are famous for their elaborate hair clips (hairstyles) that require intricate preparation.

Lifelong Friend

Dogs have a much lower life expectancy than humans, living on average for between 10 and 20 years, with smaller dogs generally having a longer life span than larger dogs. A dog's life expectancy also varies from breed to breed.

Irish Wolfhound

SHORTEST LIVING BREEDS

Breed	Average Age
Irish Wolfhound	6
Bulldog	7
Bernese Mountain Dog	7
St. Bernard	8
Great Dane	8

LONGEST LIVING BREEDS

Breed	Average Age
West Highland White Terrier	16
Border Terrier	15
Yorkshire Terrier	14
Border Collie	13
Corgi	13
Lhasa Apso	13

West Highland White Terrier

Flea

Oooo, that feels better.

Fleas running around on a dog and biting its skin will certainly irritate, and some dogs are also allergic to flea saliva.

ECTOPARASITES

Parasites that live on the outside of an animal, such as fleas and ticks, are termed ectoparasites.

+ **Fleas**—These are the bane of every pet owner's existence. If you suspect that your dog has fleas, inspect its fur and bedding for flea droppings, which look like shiny black specks. Use insecticides and flea shampoos and powders to control the fleas. Wash all bedding and treat it with insecticides immediately; this will prevent more fleas from hatching. You should also vacuum the entire home thoroughly.

+ **Ticks**—These blood-feeding parasites are often found in tall grass and shrubs, where they wait for a chance to attach to a passing host. If you spot a tick on your dog, contact a veterinarian, who will remove it from the dog's body and provide a treatment lotion.

DOG SHOW TRIALS

Dog shows award titles in a variety of categories, including:

★ **Conformation Classes**—Comparison of a dog to the breed's standard for structure and movement.

★ **Obedience and Agility Trials**—The dog is scored on its performance of specific exercises.

★ **Field Trials and Hunting or Working Tests**—The dog performs hunting and/or retrieving tasks in a simulated hunt setting.

★ **Earthdog Trials**—Small terriers and Dachshunds pursue caged rats in manmade underground tunnels.

★ **Herding Trials**—Sheep and cattle herding breeds display their skill in handling livestock.

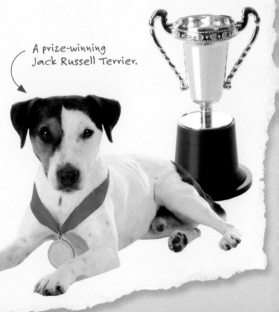

A prize-winning Jack Russell Terrier.

Harlequin Great Dane

Gibson Speaks

✦ Gibson was a harlequin Great Dane from Grass Valley, California. In 2004, he was named the world's tallest dog by Guinness World Records. He measured 42½ inches (108 cm) from shoulder to paw, and 85 inches (216 cm) when stretched out and standing on his hind legs. He weighed 180 pounds (82 kg).

✦ Gibson was a certified therapy dog, and helped to raise awareness of canine cancer before dying of the disease in 2009.

✦ The talented Gibson learned to say "I love you," and made numerous guest appearances on television, including Oprah Winfrey's talk show.

✦ Gibson co-authored his own biography, *Gibson Speaks*, with the help of owner Sandy Hall in 2008.

Illustration from 1800 showing a Turnspit running in a kitchen wheel.

WORKING BREEDS

❋ The working breeds comprise those dogs that have aided humans in many aspects of life. Over the years, these dogs were selectively bred to become experts in their job, be it guarding, pulling, or search and rescue.

❋ Most of the working breeds are large, dominant, strong dogs with courage and stamina. Most are very territorial and require a confident owner with great leadership skills.

❋ Popular working breeds include Rottweilers, Siberian Huskies, and Great Danes.

❋ Bred to work, most are happiest when they are doing the job for which they were bred, or at least when in an environment where their abilities will not go to waste.

TURNSPIT

The Turnspit was a working breed of dog with short legs and a long body, so that it would fit inside a wheel by the kitchen fire. It would run inside the wheel, which turned the roasting spit over the fire so that meat would cook evenly. The Turnspit became extinct around the mid-19th century.

Two St. Bernards resting in view of the Matterhorn in the Western Alps.

SAVIOR OF LOST TRAVELERS

☆ *Known as the Savior of Lost Travelers, the St. Bernard was bred as an alpine rescue dog— strong, sturdy, and with a short, close coat that could stand up well to the snow.*

☆ *The dog is named after the medieval Hospice of St. Bernard, situated on the St. Bernard Pass through the Western Alps between Italy and Switzerland. The hospice is named after Bernard of Menthon, the monk who founded it.*

☆ *A series of avalanches in the mid-19th century killed a large number of St. Bernards. The dogs were then interbred with Newfoundlands to increase numbers, but this resulted in a long coat that becomes weighed down with snow in alpine conditions, rendering the breed no longer suitable for alpine rescue. St. Bernards are still bred and kept in the Alps, including at the hospice, but they are no longer used for rescue work.*

"THE TAIL WAGGING THE DOG"

This phrase refers to something of minor importance being given precedence or control rather than more important factors—the tail controlling the dog, rather than the dog controlling the tail.

Coat Types

A dog's coat provides warmth, insulation, protection, and waterproofing. Coats vary enormously between breeds, from short and thin through curly to long and thick. In addition, certain characteristics may be called by different terms for different breeds, even when referring to the same thing.

DOUBLE AND SINGLE COATS

* Dogs have two different sorts of hairs: primary guard hairs and secondary hairs. The primary hairs are relatively thick, coarse, and straight. The secondary hairs are thinner, wavy, and softer.

* Double-coated dogs have an undercoat of short, soft, dense secondary hairs, and an outercoat of longer, coarser guard hairs.

* Single-coated dogs have an outercoat only.

FUR OR HAIR?
The terms are often used interchangeably, but in general, a double coat is called a fur coat, and a single coat is called a hair coat.

The Komondor's coat feels felty to the touch, and requires meticulous grooming.

KOMONDOR

The Komondor has one of the most famous coats in the dog world. Its corded coat resembles dreadlocks or a mop, and is the heaviest amount of fur in the canine world, taking almost three days to dry after a bath. When guarding sheep, the dog's fur allows it to blend in with the flock.

COLORS AND PATTERNS

Coat colors and patterns are amazingly diverse, even within the same breed. Here are a few popular combinations.

- ✤ **Brindle**—A mixture of different shades of brown and gold, producing a subtle "tiger stripe" pattern (for example, Greyhound).
- ✤ **Sable**—Black-tipped hairs on a background of gold, yellow, silver, gray, or tan (for example, German Shepherd Dog).
- ✤ **Flecked, ticked, or speckled**—Tiny specks of a different color distributed through the coat (for example, German Short-haired Pointer).
- ✤ **Spotted**—Dark spots on a light background (for example, Dalmatian).
- ✤ **Merle**—Marbled coat with irregular dark patches and spots (for example, Border Collie).
- ✤ **Harlequin**—Patches of black on a white background (for example, Great Dane).

COAT TEXTURES

Coat texture varies enormously from breed to breed. Here are a few terms commonly used.

- ✦ **Short**—Up to 1 inch (2.5 cm).
- ✦ **Long**—1 inch (2.5 cm) or longer.
- ✦ **Smooth**—Short, fine, and flat against the skin.
- ✦ **Rough**—Medium-to-long, coarse, and thick.
- ✦ **Flat**—Short, glossy, and smooth.
- ✦ **Silky**—Shiny and soft.
- ✦ **Wiry**—Stiff, harsh, and bristly; also referred to as a broken coat.
- ✦ **Curly**—Mass of thick, tight curls.
- ✦ **Wavy**—Looser curls and waves.
- ✦ **Corded**—Hairs intertwine to form dreadlocks, or cords.

Dalmatians are born white, and their famous spots appear gradually over the period of a couple of weeks.

A skijoring competition in Minneapolis.

Skijoring

+ Originating in Scandinavia, skijoring is a winter sport in which a cross-country skier is assisted by being towed by a dog or team of dogs (or sometimes a horse). The name comes from the Norwegian word *skikjøring*, meaning "ski driving."

+ Both skier and dog wear special harnesses, which are connected by a rope that is usually about 12 feet (4 m) long. There are no reins or means of controlling the dog, except by voice command.

+ Any energetic breed of dog that enjoys running and pulling can participate in skijoring, although small breeds are rare in competitions because they lack any real pulling power.

Bad Luck?

While it is generally the black cat that is considered unlucky, in some places people believe that black dogs are the ones that bring bad luck.

MONOPOLY DOG
The Scottish Terrier is the model for the dog playing piece in the board game Monopoly.

The dog lacks a collarbone, which allows it to have a greater stride length.

DOG ANATOMY

★ Modern dog breeds show more variation in physical characteristics than any other domestic animal. Apart from the number of bones in the tail, all breeds share the same skeletal structure, but variations in bone length and thickness help to produce the differences in the breeds.

★ The structure of the skeleton gives the dog the ability to run and jump quickly. Dogs' shoulder bones are not attached to the rest of the skeleton (they do not have collarbones), which gives them increased flexibility and allows for a greater stride length.

★ The skeletons of different breeds mature at different rates. The larger breeds, such as Mastiffs, can take up to a year and a half to mature, while the smaller breeds, such as toy dogs, may take only a few months.

★ The dog has a strong cardiovascular system that allows it to have good endurance but also to sprint and catch prey.

★ Dogs are natural predators and scavengers, possessing sharp teeth and strong jaws for attacking, holding, and tearing their food.

GOOD BREEDS FOR

Hot Climates
✤ Beagle
✤ Doberman Pinscher
✤ Greyhound
✤ Parson Russell Terrier
✤ Staffordshire Bull Terrier

Cold Climates
✩ Alaskan Malamute
✩ Chow Chow
✩ Newfoundland
✩ Shetland Sheepdog
✩ Siberian Husky

"Toy" Beagle

Spitz-type dogs, such as the Alaskan Malamute, were bred for cold climates. Spitz dogs are recognizable by their thick fur and pointed ears and muzzles.

CANINE QUOTES

✱ "A dog has the soul of a philosopher." *Plato*

✱ "Life is like a dogsled team. If you ain't the lead dog, the scenery never changes." *Lewis Grizzard*

✱ "Don't make the mistake of treating your dogs like humans, or they'll treat you like dogs." *Martha Scott*

✱ "If you pick up a starving dog and make him prosperous, he will not bite you. This is the principal difference between a dog and a man." *Mark Twain*

✱ "Money will buy a pretty good dog, but it won't buy the wag of his tail." *Josh Billings*

✱ "What counts is not necessarily the size of the dog in the fight; it's the size of the fight in the dog." *Dwight D. Eisenhower*

✱ "To err is human, to forgive canine." *Anonymous*

Continued on page 174

A statue of St. Roch, patron saint of dogs, at the Church of St. Augustine in Paris.

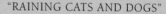

PATRON SAINT OF DOGS

St. Roch of Montpellier, France—also known as St. Rocco or St. Rock—is the patron saint of dogs. According to legend, after ministering to victims of the plague, Roch himself caught the disease and withdrew to live in a forest. While there, a dog brought him bread and healed his wounds by licking them.

"RAINING CATS AND DOGS"

This phrase is used to describe a heavy downpour of rain. The origins of the phrase are unknown, but there are many suggestions. The most widely accepted version is that the phrase originated in 17th-century England. Drainage systems were poor at that time and all sorts of waste, including the bodies of dead animals, could be found in the streets. During heavy rains, the bodies of dead cats and dogs and all sorts of other debris could be seen floating in the poorly drained, flooded areas.

WHY DO DOGS LICK FACES AND SMELL BOTTOMS?

❂ When puppies are young, they lick the muzzle of their mother to stimulate her to regurgitate food for them. While this is not necesssary for puppies born in the domestic situation, the instinct remains. It is therefore normal behavior for a dog to want to lick the faces and hands of humans, as a sign of submission and affection. You can discourage this behavior by distracting the dog with a toy. Do so gently, keeping in mind that this is already a submissive dog.

❂ Part of the way in which dogs greet each other is by sniffing. They start by sniffing each other's faces, then move around to sniff their back ends. All of this is considered proper and polite behavior among dogs, and many dogs assume it is the way they should greet people as well.

Doggy greetings at the park.

🐴 Sleeve Dogs

Very small Pekingese dogs—usually less than 6 inches (15 cm) in height—were bred for the Chinese imperial household. Members of the household would carry the dogs in the sleeves of their robes to use as handwarmers, and hence they became known as "sleeve dogs."

In the 19th century, thousands of Pekingese were kept in extraordinarily privileged circumstances in the Chinese imperial court.

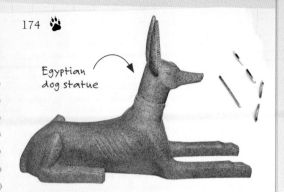

Egyptian
dog statue

Continued from page 172

Canine
Quotes

IN MOURNING

According to the 5th-century B.C. Greek historian Herodotus, members of ancient Egyptian households would shave off their hair as a way of mourning the death of a family dog.

Herodotus

* "Yesterday I was a dog. Today I'm a dog. Tomorrow I'll probably still be a dog. Sigh! There's so little hope for advancement." *Snoopy*

* "Did you ever notice when you blow in a dog's face he gets mad at you? But when you take him in a car he sticks his head out the window." *Steve Bluestone*

* "There is no psychiatrist in the world like a puppy licking your face." *Ben Williams*

* "Scratch a dog and you'll find a permanent job." *Franklin P. Jones*

* "Every dog must have his day." *Jonathan Swift*

* "Dogs laugh, but they laugh with their tails. What puts man in a higher state of evolution is that he has got his laugh on the right end." *Max Eastman*

Disk Dogs

"Disk dog" is the generic term for what is commonly called a "frisbee dog." In disk dog competitions, dogs and their human disk throwers compete in frisbee events such as distance catching and somewhat choreographed freestyle catching.

Not all dogs immediately understand the concept of frisbee—most need to be trained to catch a ball first.

Kooiker Hound

FOR THE LOVE OF DOG

✿ Surveys have shown that over 70 percent of people feel that they need to sign their dog's name on greeting cards.

✿ It is likely that just as many pet lovers include their dogs in family portraits.

✿ Over 80 percent of dog owners care enough for their pets that they buy their dog gifts for special occasions, such as birthdays.

✿ When away from home, many owners leave messages on telephone answering machines so that their dog can hear their voice while the owners are away.

✿ Studies have shown that most dog owners smile more often than non-dog owners.

✿ Many owners name their dog as the sole beneficiary in their will. In the United States alone, there have been at least 1 million dogs listed as their owner's primary beneficiary. A countess once left $106 million to her dog.

PICTURE PERFECT
The type of dog painted by Dutch artists Rembrandt and Jan Steen in the 17th century was the Kooikerhondje or Kooiker Hound.

Look! Santa Claws has been!

A pampered Cocker Spaniel.

A Cocker Spaniel communicates with other dogs in the park by scent-marking a tree.

WHY DO DOGS LIFT THEIR LEGS TO URINATE?

✤ Urine is loaded with chemical scents, so it is a source of information for dogs, telling a lot about their sex, social status, and even what they eat.

✤ When dogs lift their legs to urinate, they are leaving their scent where other dogs will smell it. They put it as high up as they can, so that it will appear that a bigger dog has been there. The best way for them to gain that extra height is to lift a leg, tilt their bodies slightly to the side, and aim for the highest spot.

✤ Dogs often share their territory, and there is an etiquette for who urinates where. A dominant dog always aims high. A more submissive dog will add its scent to the message board, but will aim lower to avoid challenging the dominant dog.

✤ An unneutered male dog may scent-mark its territory in as many as 30 locations, compared to only about three for a neutered male.

✤ Female dogs also leave chemical scents when they urinate, but they usually squat rather than lift their legs because they are not as concerned as males with marking territory or making a social display. However, dominant females do sometimes lift their legs.

BIG EARS

The Basset Hound is famous for its very short legs and extremely long ears. Bred as a scent hound, the short legs keep the dog close to the scent on the ground. The pendulous ears brush the earth, helping to stir up and capture the scent for its powerful nose to follow. Basset Hounds have been recorded as having ears measuring around a foot (30.5 cm) long.

Basset Hound

FÉDÉRATION CYNOLOGIQUE INTERNATIONALE

☆ The Fédération Cynologique Internationale (FCI) is a Belgium-based organization created in 1911 to promote and protect the science and breeding of purebred dogs across the world.

☆ It recognizes only one governing organization (such as a national kennel club) in each country.

☆ The FCI is not a registry; its purpose is to coordinate dog shows in member countries, to record show results, and to regulate judges at FCI shows. It does not set breed standards, but generally adopts the standard of a breed's country of origin—for example, the FCI recognizes the American Kennel Club breed standard for the Boston Terrier, and the (British) Kennel Club breed standard for the English Springer Spaniel.

LEONINE LEONBERGER

The German town of Leonberg had a lion on its coat of arms. The mayor, Heinrich Essig, decided to create a dog that resembled the lion and would be symbolic of the town. By crossbreeding the St. Bernard, Pyrenean Mountain Dog, and Newfoundland, he eventually developed a most handsome and friendly breed that they called the Leonberger.

It may have been designed to look like a big cat, but the Leonberger has a great love of water.

Kennels should provide good-quality shelter and comfortable bedding. You should also be encouraged to bring some of your dog's favorite toys.

BOARDING KENNELS

Sometimes it is not possible to travel with a dog—for example, if you are going abroad or staying somewhere that does not allow pets. Most people leave their dog with a friend, relative, or dog sitter. If you decide to leave your dog in a boarding kennel, here are some points to consider.

❶ Ask friends, family, and any dog owners you know if they can recommend a particular boarding kennel. Ask if they thought the kennel was clean and well organized, and respected any special requests made regarding their dog's food or housing. Did their dog come home safe and sound, with no behavioral problems or unwanted guests like fleas?

❷ Then make an unannounced stop at the boarding kennel and ask to see the facilities on offer. The staff should not find your arrival disturbing,

and should be happy to show you around. Make sure that the kennels are clean, and that all dogs look in good condition and happy. They should have access to clean water and good bedding.

❸ Well-run kennels will check for fleas when dogs arrive and just before they go home; flea problems are immediately treated. They require that all dogs have up-to-date vaccinations, including for kennel cough.

❹ Kennels should also allow you to bring food or toys from home, and provide

canned food instead of dry when asked, for instance.

❺ Leave a contact number, as well as that of your veterinarian and a trusted friend, just in case anything happens while you are away.

Flyball

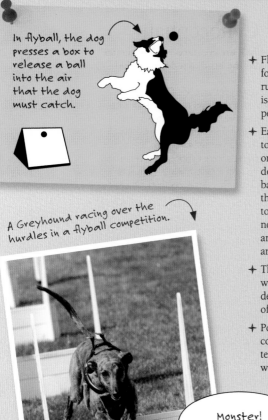

In flyball, the dog presses a box to release a ball into the air that the dog must catch.

A Greyhound racing over the hurdles in a flyball competition.

+ Flyball is a popular team sport for dogs. Teams consist of four dogs running in relay. The winning team is the one that finishes first, after penalties have been taken into account.

+ Each dog runs from the start line toward a box, jumping over hurdles on the way. On reaching the box, the dog has to activate a trigger so that a ball is released into the air. The dog then catches the ball and takes it back to the start line, at which point the next dog in the team sets off. Penalties are incurred for dropping the ball and for dogs setting off too early.

+ The course consists of four hurdles, with the hurdle height being determined by the shoulder height of the smallest dog in the team.

+ Popular breeds that compete in flyball competitions are Border Collies and terriers, although any dog breed is welcome to enter.

Monster! Help!

SCAREDY DOG?

+ *Some dogs are afraid of other animals. The most common animals are cats, other dogs, and any animals they are not familiar with.*

+ *Dogs are often afraid of things that make loud noises, such as vacuum cleaners and lawn mowers.*

+ *Most indoor dogs fear thunderstorms, because of the noise and vibrations. Some are also afraid of snow or rain.*

Cynocephali

Cynocephali are creatures with a human body and the head of a dog or jackal.

+ Anubis, the Egyptian god of the dead, was depicted with the head of a jackal. During mummification, some of the body's organs were placed in four canopic jars, with each jar's contents protected by a god. Two of the protective gods were cynocephali. Duamutef had the head of a jackal, while Hapi was represented with a dog-faced baboon head.

+ St. Christopher is sometimes depicted with the head of a dog. According to legend, he was one of a race of cannibalistic dog-headed men. After being baptised and devoting his life to the Christian faith, he was rewarded with a human head.

+ In the 5th century, a Buddhist missionary named Hui-Shen returned to China from the land of Fusang, which he described as an island of dog-headed men. Fusang has been identified as either Japan or the Americas.

Canopic jar featuring the jackal-headed god Duamutef.

Anubis, who protected the dead on their way to the underworld, was associated with the jackal because he existed in the shadows between life and death.

PHARAOH HOUND

Despite its name, there is no definite link between the Pharaoh Hound and Egypt. However, the breed does closely resemble the likenesses of dogs carved on the tomb walls of Egyptian pharaohs. In 1935, archeologists working in the great cemetery west of the pyramid of Cheops, at Giza, found an inscription recording that such a dog, named Abuwtiyuw, had beeen buried with all the ritual ceremony of a great man of Egypt by order of the kings of Upper and Lower Egypt. It is thought that Phoenician traders took these hounds to Malta and Gozo, now considered to be the Pharaoh Hound's native home.

Pharaoh Hound

Good Omen

If you see three white dogs, it is considered to be good luck.

PEDIGREE

♣ A pedigree is a record of a dog's ancestors: sire (father), dam (mother), grandsire, granddam, great-grandsire, and so forth.

♣ Dog registry agencies, such as kennel clubs, record the dog's name and pedigree information. They issue a registration certificate indicating that the dog's information is kept on file in the organization's records.

♣ Registration records include the dog's name, color, sex, parentage, date of birth, breeder, and owner, and any titles the dog has won in any shows or trials.

TOP DOG

★ According to registration statistics, the Labrador Retriever is the most popular breed of dog in the world, consistently making it into the top ten in national kennel club statistics, and achieving the number one spot in many countries.

★ Labradors do not come from Labrador. They come from Newfoundland, Canada, where fishermen used the dogs to help land their nets. The dogs are thought to have originated in Devon, England, and to have been taken to North America by fishermen. In the 1830s, Newfoundland fishermen reimported the dogs into England, and it is these dogs that formed the basis of the breed as we know it.

★ Labrador Retrievers are affectionate and loving, and great with children. Exuberant in youth, they are easy to train, and often work as guide dogs for the blind.

The Labrador Retriever makes an ideal family pet, but needs plenty of exercise and regular brushing.

Ancient History

+ The ancient Greek poet Homer immortalized the dog as man's most faithful companion in his epic poem the *Odyssey* around 850 B.C.

+ The earliest recorded history of dogs was written by the Greek historian Xenophon (c. 430–354 B.C.). His treatise, called *Cynegeticus* ("Hunting with Dogs"), was devoted to hunting and hunting dogs.

+ In his *Systema Naturae* ("The Order of Nature"), published in 1735, Swedish naturalist Carolus Linnaeus was the first person to classify dogs as anything other than workers.

A 1-year-old dog is roughly 10½ years old in human years.

Ancient Greek poet Homer wrote about the dog as man's best friend.

HOW OLD IS YOUR DOG?

★ It is often said that one dog year equals seven human years. This is a quick and easy way of converting a dog's age to its human equivalent, but it is only a rough approximate.

★ Dogs reach adulthood earlier than humans, so a more accurate formula is to equate one dog year to 10½ human years for the first two years. Then for each subsequent year, equate one dog year to four human years.

★ Even this is not completely accurate, however, because it also depends on the breed and size of the dog. Different breeds mature at different rates, and smaller breeds reach their full size earlier than larger dogs.

Ancient Greeks and Romans spread nets for hunting, and used dogs to drive prey into the nets.

A barking dog can be intimidating, so be considerate to the mail carrier and keep the dog safely confined.

DOGS AND THE MAIL CARRIER

✱ Many dogs make a big fuss and bark at the mail carrier. Despite this, the dog more than likely does not have anything personal against the mail carrier. The dog is just looking after its territory. In fact, most dogs have a little watchdog in them. This trait is inherited from their ancestors, who had to defend their territories and limited food supplies from prying paws.

✱ Most dogs have an instinctive urge to protect their territory, but another reason they make such a big deal is due to anticipation. Dogs like routines, and because the mail comes every day at more or less the same time, it becomes part of their routine.

✱ Mail carriers, meter readers, parcel couriers, and any other strangers who purposely head up to the house and then look as though they are retreating when they get barked at are going to get the same reception.

 FLOWER DOG

American artist Jeff Koons created *Puppy* in 1992, a 43-foot (12.4 m) high floral sculpture of a West Highland White Terrier. The steel substructure contains an irrigation system and supports around 70,000 fresh flowers. The dog stands outside the Guggenheim Museum in Bilbao, Spain.

"Puppy" by Jeff Koons has become a symbol of Bilbao, Spain.

Grooming Tips

Most dogs love being groomed, especially if they are accustomed to it from puppyhood. It is a time when they have the owner's sole attention, and it can be a pleasant and relaxing experience for both dog and owner.

+ Groom dogs from the back end toward the front (the opposite direction to stroking), and upward at the sides and chest. Tails are a sensitive area in some dogs, so take care when brushing this part. Finish each grooming session by brushing the coat in the direction the fur lies.

+ There are several different types of grooming brush. Wire pin brushes are good for long-haired dogs, such as Collies, and rubber brushes for short-haired dogs, such as Labrador Retrievers. Thin-haired dogs need gentle brushing with a bristle brush.

+ Wire-haired breeds have harsh outer coats and thick, soft undercoats. In addition to brushing, these breeds' coats need to be professionally stripped (dead hair removed) every six to eight weeks.

I may be small, but I need a lot of grooming to get my coat this silky.

HIS MASTER'S VOICE

When his dog Nipper died in 1895, English painter Francis Barraud used a photograph of the terrier staring intently at a phonograph as the basis for a painting. Modifying the painting to show a gramophone, he sold both the painting and the rights to the title "His Master's Voice" to the Gramophone Company. Brands that have used Nipper's logo and His Master's Voice slogan include HMV, RCA, and JVC.

The Australian Silky Terrier requires regular bushing and combing. Lots of attention to its coat is essential if it is to compete in the show ring.

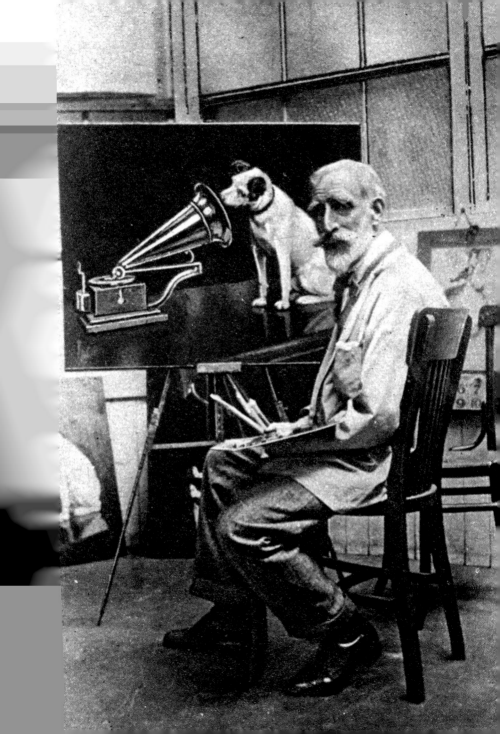

Index

Credits

Dedication
For Jackson. A dog who changed
my life. A best friend forever.
Never forgotten.

Author's Acknowledgments
Thanks go to my wonderful dogs,
Chloe and Mia, for reminding me
on a daily basis that life and the
world is never more fun than in
the time spent sniffing a single
blade of grass for a full five
minutes. My wife, Kim, for
doing the hard work that enables
me to indulge in books like this.
Jennifer White for doing a fine
job in helping turn the words
into something more legible to
human eyes, and to everyone—
friends, family, colleagues—
whose efforts and support enable
me to have the greatest job on
earth, writing about dogs with
my own canine friends. Finally,
a tip of the hat to Jackson, my
first dog and the inspiration
for an entire adult life spent
dedicated to all things canine.
Thank you all.

Picture Credits
Hulton-Deutsch Collection/
Corbis *page 40*; Everett
Collection/Rex Features *page 58*;
HO Davis/The Kobal Collection
page 90; GTV Archive/Rex
Features *page 113 (below)*; Mary
Evans Picture Library *page 126*;
Bettmann/Corbis *page 137*;
c.SND/Everett/Rex Features
page 145 (above); Corbis *page
152 (below)*; TopFoto *page 185*.

While every effort has been made
to credit contributors, Quarto
would like to apologize should
there have been any omissions or
errors—and would be pleased to
make the appropriate correction
for future editions of the book.